Stealing German Bread

03-26-09

Stealing German Bread

Yocheved Artzi MS LMFT

To order additional copies of this book, contact:
Xlibris Corporation
1-888-795-4274
www.Xlibris.com
Orders@Xlibris.com
53796

Contents

In memory of my grandparents, the Moshkovitz family, Yocheved and all victims of racial hatred.

Preface

As a child I was not allowed to ask my mother, Rachel, any questions about the horror she experienced in Auschwitz. I was born only six years after the Holocaust, and my mother's pain was too raw to be revealed. We all learned about the tragedy of our nation in school in Israel. There were many stories and books and Holocaust memorial days that were very informative. But I wanted to hear it from my mother. I wanted to know what really happened to her; her own particular story.

With every book that I read about the holocaust I found myself wondering, "is that what happened to my Mom? How did she look when she was standing in line for selection? Was she skinny like those women in my 6th grade history book? Is that how my grandfather looked like when he was herded to the gas chambers?"

In the city that I grew up in Israel I was surrounded with neighbors, family and friends, survivors that were talking about the horror, but never in my language, Hebrew. What ever they said about their lost families and their longing was said in either Yiddish or Hungarian. It was a common custom for the survivors to speak in their old language so that the children would not understand.

The only thing that Mom was able to share was her pain of losing her entire family in Auschwitz, and that she was starving to death in the concentration camps. I was always encouraged to finish all the food on my plate because people starved to death in concentration camps.

And, "God forbidden," we were not allowed to throw away food even when it was rotten. Food was very precious. Food was the main source of life in our home.

Another thing that I learned from my mother then was that she was hoping that one day, someone would document her testimony. Her dream was that somebody would write her story so that "the world will learn what happened there." But she could never find an inner strength to tell it to anybody.

Fortunately, my mother's silence was broken sixty years after the war, when my family and I moved to America. My mother felt more comfortable to reveal her stories through our daily trans-Atlantic telephone calls. She unfolded her horrific testimony in historical order, what happened day after day. She lived for our daily transatlantic conversations. She was content to know that I would write her story in the English language so that my American friends and clients would be able to read it in their own language.

This book reveals my mother's personal experience of surviving the most horrific human experience, as well her daughter's personal reactions and memories of growing up with a mother's courage.

The story also reveals my mother's extraordinary ability to overcome the hunger, the humiliation and the brutality that was inflicted by other human beings. My mother's strength sprang from a deep need to sustain her beloved sister, Yocheved's, life.

For my mother, the only thing that mattered was to protect Yocheved who grew increasingly sick and weak during a year of imprisonment in concentration camps.

And for me, and my children, we are very thankful to my mother who was, finally, able to share her invaluable, first—person view into the atrocity of the Holocaust.

A special thanks is given to my friend and editor, Ms. Shelba Sellers, who helped in writing this story in English and edited the manuscript several times with much patience and love.

Yocheved Artzi MS LMFT
Thomasville Georgia, 2008

Selection

It is my mother
Who standing naked
In Hungarian Jewish line
A beloved sister is waiting
On the other side

Only a few hours past
They were torn apart
From a loving family
Passing through a gate
Of a perilous town

Thrown away from homes
Into rushing lines
To an unknown destiny
Herded in a cattle car

Their elders gone
Into ashen clouds

Gushing into smoking sky
Of weeping clouds

My mother naked waiting
To a fate decree!
To the right?
To the left?
Awaiting her sister's fate?

On top of line
A pointing "doctor"
Cutting, stamping women's fate!
To life or death!

A beloved sister's body is now in test
In a vicious doctor's hand
"Looking healthy"
He forthright
Pointing to the right!

**From the collection of poetry, *I Have two Countries*,
Written and translated from Hebrew by**
Yocheved Artzi MS LMFT

1

The Dream

She had another comforting dream, painful and yet comforting, one of those dreams that sustained her sanity years after the war. A dream of a family, of love that helped her to survive the hell of Auschwitz.

Mom breathed deeply and dived into a recurrent dream of a lost world. We were preparing for the Sabbath on a cool evening in 1942. I was helping my mother, Deborah, to serve the Shabbat dinner. I lit the white candles, covered my eyes with ten fingers, and blessed the Shabbat, *she said. Mom's memories of her happy family life in Hungary became a dream she could revisit at night.*

My father, Rabbi Meier, and brothers just arrived from the synagogue, *Mom continued.* We served the traditional Friday night meal: fish, chicken soup, noodles, challah bread, and a homemade wine. My lovely sister, Yocheved, was standing at my side, pouring the wine into Father's silver goblet. Father chanted the lovely Shabbat hymn, "Shalom aliechem malachi hashalom . . ." And then it was darkness, my family was gone, disappeared, and only my sister and I were standing, alone, in Block 13 in Auschwitz.

It all started when I moved to America. Sixty years of silence ends with the help of geographical distancing. Mom tells me about the horrors of Auschwitz through our daily phone conversation from Israel. Mom is sitting on her bed in the nursing home in Tel Aviv, and I am in the kitchen in Thomasville, Georgia, a small Southern town thousand miles away.

Her willingness to talk now seems to be part of her "growing older" that allows Mom's heart to open and unfold the story—the forbidden tale about which I was never allowed to ask, to hear. You can read in books, you will learn in school, *she promised me when I begged her to tell me about the tragedy. I was young, and her pain was too raw. She never felt comfortable talking about her pain in the concentration camps in front of her naïve innocent children. Somehow, she knew that describing her ordeal would make us very sad.*

Sixty years after the war, she tells over and over the same stories. She lives for our daily stories, for the daily transatlantic talks, and she can't tell it enough. She talks, and I write. She gets headaches, and I get longing aches to be with my mother and to return to my homeland, to go back to my former life in Israel.

I moved to Budapest at the age of twenty-five or twenty-six—*Mom did not remember exactly.* The big-city adventure was a dream, and my parents protested, "A Jewish young woman alone? In the big city?" My father worried. But I knew in my heart what I wanted to do, and I did not conform despite Father's objections. My father, Rabbi Meier Moshkovitz, as he was known, was a distinguished rabbi in our small Hungarian town of Sighet. He spoke several languages and encouraged his children to do the same. But on the other hand, Father thought that I, a young Jewish woman, should stay at home until I would find the right husband.

I left the small town and traveled to Budapest without query, leaving behind a loving family and childhood friends. I wanted a new life.

I found a job and a small apartment on my first day in the city. A friend from Sighet introduced me to her landlord, a kind Hungarian man whose family owned a small bread store. I rented an apartment from him and worked in his family bread store, selling fresh bread and buns.

Delighted to earn money, I saved some and sent packages of food to my family, fulfilling a dream. The clerk in the post office loved my visits. He learned my family address in Sighet by heart. I sent two boxes of rice, two boxes of potatoes, and two boxes of flour every single month. The clerk was impressed. "A young woman sending food to her family, what a dedication." My mom, Deborah, was proud. "My daughter is managing well in the big city." But she was also ashamed of the need of assistance. For Mom, it was the "parents who should send food to their children, and not the other way around." Who would have believed then of what would become of our lives in such short time.

My father was concerned about my spiritual life in the big city, asking himself and my mother, "Is she keeping kosher? Is she observing the Jewish holidays?" He sent me letters, reminding me of upcoming holidays, of religious obligations, and Jewish deeds. He even sent a family friend, a relative from Sighet who lived in Budapest, to check my living condition—my lifestyle. My parents learned to trust me and even enjoyed the financial assistance. They needed it. Times were rough. My brother-in-law, like most young Hungarians, was drafted into the Hungarian army, and my sister, Blanca (his wife), and her two young children returned home to live with my parents.

Life changed forever within few short months. On March 19, 1944, German forces invaded Hungary, and life for the Jews altered. The German regime replaced the Hungarian prime minister Kelly with the general Dome Sztojay, a frantically pro-German that quickly agreed to deport all the Jews from Hungary.

Life in Budapest became unbearable. Jews were fired from their jobs and begun to feel the stormy wind of hatred.

I was fired from my job. One early morning, two government agents stormed the bakery, asking the store managers whether he had any

Jewish workers. The owner, to his naiveté, denied it immediately. The two agents looked at me, asking for verification. My heart was beating rapidly. I knew it was my end at the store. "I am Jewish," my lips blurted proudly. The agents' faces turned dark, and the storeowner shrunk with fear. Jews were not allowed to serve the Hungarian public nor to touch or sell bread—it was "God forbidden." The hope that the Hungarian government would remain loyal to their Jewish citizens evaporated, and the hope that the war would be over before the Germans arrived in Hungary was gone.

A wave of tales about concentration camps, gas chambers, and mass murders in Poland and Germany flooded the air. It did not make sense. People talked about death camps and gas chambers, but we did not believe any of these rumors. Germany was far away from us, we thought then. Such terrors would not happen to us good citizens, so we, the Hungarian Jews, believed.

A refugee couple, who were Polish Jews, provided an eyewitness account of the horrors in Germany and Poland. I found them wandering in the streets of Budapest, a few blocks from my house, walking on the sidewalk. A confused young couple, a man and woman in their late twenties, almost my age. Dirty, worn-out, covered with skin rash. They were speaking Polish and Yiddish—the common language of the European Jews. Their unkempt appearance and use of Polish language endangered their lives. Foreigners were not allowed on the Hungarian land.

Thinking of my Jewish deeds, I offered them refuge in my apartment.

Only a small number of Polish Jews were able to escape the horror in Poland. Some had little money and luck, and others had good connections, *Mom clarified.* The Polish couple arrived in Budapest, paying their way out with gold jewelry. They hid in forests, barns, and farmers' backyards, buying and stealing food.

They revealed the horror of Hitler's plan, to end up the "Jewish Dilemma," to finish with the Jews, to kill them all.

The couple, hidden in a forest, eye-witnessed the terror, the dismay, the horror before their own eyes. They saw a mass killing of Jews in a small town in Poland. The Jews in the small village were handed hoes and were forced to dig a large ditch and to bury their family, friends, neighbors, children, babies, one after one. There were shooting, body parts scattering, bodies collapsing, and shouting, the young couple told.

The gravediggers were buried last. Nobody resisted. The Germans stood aside, yelling orders. Nobody protested.

The Polish villagers were helping the Germans and hurrying the process. They were pushing bodies into the freshly dug graves. The Jewish couple saw it all, an impossible story to believe, *Mom added.*

It could only happen in Poland, or so we thought. It would not happen here in our beautiful cultured country, Hungary, we comforted ourselves then before it all happened.

The couple was in terrible health, covered with scabies, a contagious irritating skin disease. I medicated them with natural home remedies including soothing cream that a Jewish doctor gave me. He did not know about my secret—the hidden couple—and did not ask also. Doctors were not allowed to help Jews and refugees. The couple stayed in my apartment for a few months until the arrival of the bad news.

It was in April 1944. The Hungarian army ordered the Jews that lived outside of Budapest to move into ghettos, into closed neighborhoods in segregated section of a town. For me, the declaration of the ghettos marked the end of life in the big city. I had no purpose in continuing to live safely in the big city. My family was in danger. I needed to rescue them, my parents in Sighet, in anyway possible.

I took the night train from Budapest directly to Sighet, my hometown. Traveling at night was safer. Jews were prohibited from public places and not allowed into public transportation. The train was crowded with Hungarians, city people, and villagers.

I sat in a side seat, did not look any passengers in the eye, and kept my head down as low as possible, avoiding any eye contact, fearing the worst. Shrinking my back into a jacket, I covered my head with a hat, almost invisible.

The Jewish couple was right—they told the truth. Bad things were going to happen.

Mom needed a break. She still feels guilty of her inability to save her family, feeling guilty for surviving the horror, for living. She is still wondering, in her late eighties, whether she did enough or if she could have done more.

No matter how often I remind Mom, "You did your best" and that her parents were happy to see her even for a little while before they were all deported to the gas chambers, Mom still questions, "Why did I survive?" and "Did I do enough?"

It is teatime in Mom's nursing home. She hangs up the phone and leaves the room to join her friends—elderly people like her, other Holocaust survivors. I imagine Mom walking in the hallway, and I feel her longing for the closeness of family once again.

2

Back to Sighet

My life in the big city did not matter anymore, *Mom continued the following morning, picking up exactly where she left off in her story the day before.* My parents did not know that I was coming.

The train arrived in Sighet at dawn. The town was surrounded by German soldiers. The train station was covered with German officers and Hungarian police. The German Gestapo, spotless in their ironed clothing, were frightening in their black leather boots, carrying guns, and leading vicious dogs.

It was scary. The Germans invaded my hometown, and it was dangerous to continue home. Big posters on the train station walls prohibited Jews from using public transportation.

The Hungarian police, the gendarme, controlled the train station entrances and exits. The German officers stood outside, watching the Hungarian police enforcing the new Nazis orders. The Hungarian soldiers checked the passengers' papers, passenger after passenger, family after family, children, and the elderly. They all had to show their documents to verify their identity.

It was frightening. I did not have any identification papers, and I was Jewish. My fate was determined. I was afraid to leave the train, but there was no time to hesitate. Pushed down to the train platform into the crowd, and I was moved forward. I walked behind a Hungarian family, a grandfather and grandmother with a young couple and their three young children. Noticing my intention, they allowed me to assimilate among them. The father checked my steps, observed my body head to toe while continuing to walk silently. The family had just returned home from the big city, carrying baskets with goods. They walked naturally, busy with their own business, feeling my presence, but still ignoring the danger. They kept walking. I walked in between the grandfather, an old man with a hunchback, and his elderly wife. I touched his arm lightly. They were not Jewish. They were safe, and I passed in between them unnoticed.

My parents were thrilled to see me. They were not surprised. They knew that as soon as the news of the Germans' invasion of Sighet would spread, I would return home. I adjusted to life at home quickly just as if I never left to go to the big city.

My parents, like other Jews, were prepared for the worst, for the upcoming unknown. At the outside, life seemed casual—children playing in front yards, mothers buying groceries and cooking, fathers busying with their tasks—but inside their hearts, there was tremendous fear. The Jews were worrying about the next new Nazi ordinance. The Germans and the Fascist Hungarians enacted new decrees daily, making life impossible.

All synagogue doors were closed. Praying and practicing Judaism was forbidden. My father, Meier Moshkovitz, a well-recognized melamed, continued his Hebrew and Bible teaching hidden in a back room at our house. He was a melamed, a rabbi teaching young children to read the Torah and write Hebrew. A great disciplinarian and educator, my father was admired by his pupils and their parents. My father did not succumb to the new rules and continued his teaching despite the German prohibition. My responsibility was to watch the street from the window to alert the family of an incoming danger from Hungarian guardsmen.

Our home turned to an underground synagogue. Neighbors and family members continued to study in the hidden room.

Within a few days of my arrival, the Jews of Sighet were rounded up and dispatched into concentrated ghettos.

Our street, the Serpent Street, like its name says, was long and narrow, shaped as a snake. *Mom does not skip an opportunity to describe her loveable childhood street.* The Serpent Street turned into a designated ghetto, the largest ghetto for the Jews of Sighets—my wonderful hometown.

The extended family—aunts, uncles, and cousins—that lived on the other side of town were forced to move into the ghetto on Serpent Street. They joined our family and moved into the house. Every house on the street turned into a shelter for relatives and strangers. Life at home changed. It was crowded, and the more people in the house, the quieter it became, a strange silence.

My mother, Deborah, kept busying herself with household chores—more cooking, more sewing, preparing things for the unknown. My oldest sister, Blanca, twenty-two years old, had just returned home with her two young children, little Judah, a two-year-old, and Ressie, a four-year-old. They moved back home when Blanca's husband, Moses, was forced into the service of the Hungarian army. He was recruited into the army a few months prior to my arrival, and we never heard from him thereafter.

My family life changed. There was no place for self-pity, or for a future plan. We were only worried about the present. We searched for cheap food sources and low-cost flour. We baked breads to feed the new mouths in the house. We cooked soups to quiet the rumbling stomachs, continuing with a daily existence. There was fear in my mother's eyes and a look of terror on my father's face. I did not want to add to their suffering, so I kept my fear within, pound inside as if a rope tied in knots.

Jews were forbidden from leaving the ghetto. The Hungarian army guarded the ghetto, the gates, and the streets. The Germans supervised the Hungarians, verifying the enforcement of the new regulations. The Germans did not get involved in the daily policing. Only individuals with special permission were allowed to get in or out of the perimeters of enclosure.

Jews had to wear yellow star badges, and those that "forgot" to wear them were beaten to death and not seen in the ghetto anymore.

I remember this yellow star. Mom kept it all these years after the war. She hid it in her closet drawer along with other prisoner clothes from Bergen-Belsen. She hid it in the bottom of the drawer. It was her secret, and mine too.

We never talked about it, but it was fascinating. The relics enticed my imagination, and as soon as Mom left home to work, my hands traveled deep into the drawer, searching for the yellow star. I pulled it out. It was made of a silky piece of cloth, painfully smooth. I put it on my shirt, on the left side, on my heart, just as it looked in the picture in my history book, the yellow star of my mother.

Mom never knew about my secret, my attraction to the memorabilia from the war in the deep drawer. And she still does not know to this day. The yellow star and other items were given to Yad Vashem, the Israeli Holocaust Museum, when mother moved to the nursing home.

Soon after our relatives moved into the ghettos, Jewish men were ordered to shave their beards, thereby erasing all of their Jewish identity and exposing cheeks that had never been shaved before.

My father had to shave his long beard and cut his sidelock, and that was unbearable.

He shaved his face. There was no other choice, but he could not tolerate the shame. He covered his face with Mom's babushka, a female kerchief, a woman's head cover. Father would keep his eyes lowered down, and I could not direct my eyes into his face. It was impossible to witness the pain. My powerless father. Seeing him that way was heartbreaking.

The youngest grandchildren, Judah and Ressie, played with friends in the yard. They felt the stress and the fear but continued to enjoy life in their own childish way.

Nobody could imagine how fast the end would come, *Mom paused.* The Jewish couple was right. They talked about the upcoming evil, but we refused to hear.

I did not tell my parents about the story of the Polish couple, I was afraid to share. My parents heard horrible stories as well about concentration camps and gas chambers, but they did not talk about it either. Terrifying stories were running through everybody's mind and stayed there, an unspeakable fear.

The Germans' annihilation of the Jews in the small polish town began with killing the youngest first and ending with adults. *Mom repeated,* they shot them at once.

Mom is getting a headache, one of those terrible headaches that come along with painful stories. Mom is asking the nurse for her headache medication through the intercom in her room.

Üdvözlet Szegedröl.   Zsinagóga

Picture postcard showing an exterior view of the synagogue in Seghed Hungary

3

Deportation

It was a hot night. We could not sleep quietly, *Mom continued her story the following afternoon. She was feeling better and wanted to tell more and more. She wanted the world to know what happened there.*

Orders were thrown into the air, in the street, and into the yards and open doors and windows early in the morning before dawn. Shouts in Hungarian, Yiddish, and German shook the hearts of the weary. Loud voices yelled, "Hurry up! Get ready! Deportation!"

We were awakened by Hungarian officers slamming doors, knocking windows, and breaking furniture. We jumped quickly out of beds feeling anguish and impending doom. The Hungarian officers armed with rifles and with sticks entered houses, ordering people to leave their homes. Fear and desperation paralyzed the hearts of all who heard the orders.

"You must leave your house now," our next-door neighbor, a Jewish-mandated policeman, yelled in Yiddish. "You are allowed to take only one bag with little food." Only one bag of food, *Mom repeated.*

The real moment was coming. The Jewish local police assisted the Hungarians, barking orders and directions. The Jewish police force was created to mediate and to communicate between the Hungarians, the Germans, and the Jews in the ghetto, *Mom clarified the history.*

I looked at my parents. They were terrified. We had to leave, to evacuate, to desert our home, carrying one small bag, each person with one small bag only.

We had only a few hours to prepare to get ready for the unknown. "What should we put in the bag?" *Mom asked again, now many years after her challenging order, still questioning herself and questioning me as if she was reliving those moments again while telling the story to me, her daughter.*

My mother was prepared. She knew that this moment would come. She had several cloth bags already made. She had her supplies ready. She knew something bad was going to happen but did not talk about it.

I filled my bag with a few pieces of bread, boiled eggs, a small piece of cake, and apples. I helped my sister, Yocheved, to pack her bag. She had few pieces of dried meat, and we planed to share.

The children held my hands. Little Judah was searching for comfort—he was terrified—and little Ressie was shedding tears silently. The children were scared. They felt our shaking as if they knew that the end was coming.

I felt numb and could say nothing. I was just there ready for the worst. My father was busy hiding his precious books, his prayer books, and Bibles. He was also prepared just as my mother was. He carved a niche in the wall a few weeks earlier, and we did not know it. It was a niche in a wall in the back room—a well-hidden niche—to hide his holy books, the Sefrie Kodesh. He covered the books with layers of bricks. Father was prepared too, and he was sure that the journey to the unknown would end soon. He did not want anybody to touch his holy books while he was gone.

And I found his books when I returned home after it was all over, *Mom sighed deeply*. They were untouched. The neighbors that occupied our house after we were deported did not find the books behind the bricks.

Rassel and Sorrah, my sisters, were busy packing bags silently, wondering which item would be more helpful, more important. Gedaliah, my youngest brother who had just celebrated his bar mitzvah, assisted my father. He wanted to hide his bar mitzvah books along with Father's books. Jonathan, my oldest brother, was away serving in the Hungarian army. It was mandatory service even for the Jews. The healthy Jewish men were obligated to serve in the Hungarian forces.

My father was a Zionist—*Mom was so proud with her father.* He always dreamed about the Holy Land. He dreamed of leaving Hungary and moving to Jerusalem, but my mother refused consistently. She did not want to leave her family, her relatives, her friends, the livelihood of Sighet.

And then nothing helped anymore. She had to leave it all, *Mom moaned.* We left the house as we were ordered. We left and never returned as a family.

The Serpent Street was crowded. Sidewalks, asphalt, dirt ground, were covered with families, carrying bags on backs on shoulders. Children were holding on to their parents, and older brothers and sisters holding younger siblings. Mothers were holding babies on their arms.

Families were streaming toward the end of the street and directed toward the big synagogue. The Hungarian officers yelled hysterically, pushing the weak and the elderly, shoving those that interfered with the quick pace. The Hungarians wanted everyone to move fast.

Children were crying. They felt the upcoming danger ahead. Mothers were holding babies on their arms, walking with the flow silently, terrified. Fathers were holding hands with their sons. We stood in the front yard waiting for the next order to the unknown.

I was astonished at Mom's recollection. She revealed detail after detail. Painful, intense memories rose to the surface. Is it too much? Should we stop the story now? The conversation was getting heavier, and I changed the subject to talks about the rummy, Mom's favorite card game. She plays rummy every night. This was her way to relax the pain all these years. But she did not hear me. She was embedded in the Serpent Street, walking with her family toward the big synagogue, re-experiencing the horror.

We were ordered to stop at the Jewish synagogue in the front yard, the beautiful old building that had served the Jewish community for many years. The synagogue with the Sefrie Torah, the holy antique Bibles, and the menorah with its the seven silver candle holders that made our holidays so special, the synagogue that was the home for celebrations, holidays, and happiness was now witnessing the shame and the misery of our German persecution.

The Hungarians commanded us to stand in line, and we lined up, one after one, a long line of human convoy. The weather was hot, and we were thirsty, but there was no water. Children cried. They needed water, and nobody could help them.

The Gypsies, our neighbors, were standing there. They came to watch the shame. They stood aside, and they laughed at our shame. Pointing fingers as we passed by, the Gypsies were thrilled with the Jewish despair. They seemed overjoyed and satisfied with our defeat.

And we met the Gypsies again a few days later in Auschwitz, *Mom revealed.* Their fate was no different. The Gypsies were decimated just as the Jews were, maybe even faster. The Nazis had a plan for them also, *Mom sighed. She did not forget the shame of the Gypsies' betrayal.*

In contrast to the Hungarians, the Jews lived peacefully with the Gypsies before the Germans' invasion. We respected them, bought merchandise from them, listened to their sidewalk singers. The Hungarians did not like the Gypsies. Gypsies were considered outsiders in the Hungarian society. They worked mostly for the Jews. *Mom emphasized the absurdity.* How could they laugh at our misfortune? But they did not laugh for long. We had the same destiny. We met them soon after . . . in Auschwitz. They were gone first, even before the Jews. *Mom was getting tired. The story about the Gypsies saddened her. I felt it in her voice. It gets softer, almost disappearing.*

The Hungarian officers searched our bags, *Mom continued the following morning.* We were allowed to carry only a few pieces of food. The Hungarian gendarmes searched for forbidden items and found them. They turned bags upside down, threw precious items into large piles—a pile of prayer books, of shawls, of socks, of sweaters, of jewelry, of hats, and of other precious items that were needed to survive. They found my mom's hidden prayer book and threw it into a pile of books. They found my sister's golden wedding ring; it was thrown into a large bag of valuable items.

Soon the search was over. The human motorcade—mothers, fathers, children, and babies—continued toward the train station with dragging feet. We were thirsty, hungry, and exhausted. Thoughts of sitting and resting the aching feet were only a dream.

The short loud gray locomotive carrying cattle wagons arrived at the station. We were tired and careless. There was nothing on our minds but a small hope for a spot to sit down in the wagon, waiting for the unknown.

The German Gestapo took over. We were handed into the arms of the beast, *Mom clarified.* The real suffering had just started.

View of the kitchen barracks, the electrified fence, and the gate at the main camp of **Auschwitz (Auschwitz** I). In the foreground is the sign "Arbeit Macht Frei" (Work makes one free).

Date: 1945
Locale: Auschwitz, [Upper Silesia] Poland; Birkenau; **Auschwitz** III; Monowitz; **Auschwitz** II
Credit: USHMM, courtesy of Instytut Pamieci Narodowej
Copyright: Agency Agreement

4

The Journey

The SS counted the people, preparing for the voyage. There were too many people for a small cattle wagon. Only eighty were allowed into a wagon that was suited for six to eight cows or horses.

I was scared. I was not ready yet to separate from my family. We wanted to continue to the unknown together. And we were lucky. The family remained together. We were grouped and pushed into the same wagon. The SS shouted orders, and we were herded into the wagon, pushed viciously with rifle butts.

The wagon was filled quickly with mothers, fathers, and crying children, all standing or sitting face-to-face and back-to-back. My mother, dressed in a dark long dress that covered her round figure, sat on the wagon floor and stretched out her fatigued legs. They were swollen, and I was worried about her health. My father sat on the floor too. He was exhausted but held his head proudly. There was no talking, no conversation, only minimum amount of words with a few moans and groans and babies' crying in the background.

I leaned over my sister Yocheved's back, holding my bag tightly to protect the few crumbs that were left, our lives' savior. Children cried for water, and parents were helpless. There was no fresh air—the wagon had very little narrow air openings for the cattle.

The wagons were used for transporting cattle, animals, not people, *Mom clarified again.* The air openings were too high, and only the tallest among us were able to stick their noses against the side of the wagon and breathe through the opening bars. We took turns to breathe and to watch where we were heading. The short people and children were not lucky. They were too far from the fresh air. The air inside the wagon was thick, heavy, filled with human body heat and sweat. Some lost strength and fainted. My aunt Rebecca was six months pregnant and gasping for air. She lost her strength and lay flat on the wagon floor. Her body was pushed to the corner—there was not enough space for a stretched-out body on the floor.

My grandmother Peiah died a few months earlier while I was living in Budapest and before the Germans occupied Hungary. She was ninety-six years old when she took her last breath. And in the wagon, for the first time, I was happy that she was not alive, that she did not have to feel the shame.

We fell asleep standing up, my sister's head leaning on my shoulder. We took turns, heads on shoulders, supporting and balancing each other's body, breathing in one pace, eating breadcrumbs when hunger overcame the need to "save for later." We did not know when we would receive our next nourishment or where we were heading.

My mother Deborah leaned on Blanca, my oldest sister. They were worn-out. Little Judah and Ressie napped on Blanca's lap on and off, in between crying and questioning.

People exchanged spots, moved from the right to the left to feel alive. I searched for Father and brother. I could not see them anymore. I knew that they were standing or sitting on the wagon floor somewhere. I wanted to get closer but did not have the little energy to do so. In my heart, I imagined my father praying silently with closed eyes as he always did in time of stress. My father, Meier, knew the whole prayer book by heart. And I knew that my brother Gedaliah was in good hands—he was with our father.

My cousins and aunts were sitting close by. We stayed together from the beginning. They moved to our house on Serpent Street when it turned to a ghetto and from the first moment of the deportation. We were afraid to lose each other.

Jeremiah, my cousin who was three years younger than me, could not tolerate the trap, the humiliation. He wanted to jump off the wagon at the next stop for fueling. He was desperate to live or die, but not to be trapped in the suffocating wagon. His mother, my aunt Tzeviah, was furious, not ready to lose her son. He was going to get killed by jumping or by shooting. She tried to convince him to change his decision. But he was determined to jump at the first train stop. He had it all planned out.

My aunt begged for help. She asked me to help change his mind—she knew that I was the only one to whom he would listen. I pleaded with him not to jump. I told him that things will get better, that the journey would be over soon, and that if we are all going to die anyway, we should not rush the end.

My cousin did not listen to me. He wanted to escape the torture. He was determined. But he could not jump—the air openings were too small and sealed with iron bars, and the exit doors were locked from the outside. The train continued forward with no stops for fueling, no chance for Jeremiah to jump out and to escape.

The tallest people that were able to look through the air openings kept us informed of the changing locations, the names of the villages, and the train stations. "We crossed the Hungarian border, leaving our country," somebody announced. Then it was "Czechoslovakia," "Slovakia," "South Poland." We were heading to the worst of all—to Poland. And I remembered the Jewish couple from Budapest. They told the truth, *Mom sighed deeply*. The Polish couple escaped the hell that we were heading into. They warned, but we did not want to hear. We did not do anything.

The Polish Jews ran away. They escaped the hell that we were heading to, *Mom repeated*. I could have done the same. I could have remained safe in Budapest, but I wanted to save my family. I returned home to Sighet to help my family. There was no purpose for life without my family—even if I would die with them.

"You did the best you could," I reminded Mom. "You helped your family in their last days, you returned home to be with them. They were happy to see you."

Mom kept quiet. She still feels guilty for not saving their lives. At the age of eighty-six, Mom still wonders how and what the purpose was.

And I reminded my mom that she won the war, created a new family, a new generation, daughters, grandchildren, and great-grandchildren.

Mom kept quiet. She did not hear me.

Mom does not remember how many days and nights the journey lasted, maybe three or four days. She remembers the hunger, the thirst, the fear, the confusion, the desperation, the suffocating heat.

Somebody announced, "Auschwitz." *Mom's voice broke.* We arrived in Auschwitz, a place we had not heard before, but we learned about it very fast. The train continued to move a few kilometers and then stopped. A sharp whistle cut the thick air.

I searched for my family. We huddled and stood together inside the wagon, ready, fearful. The doors were still closed. Little Judah and little Ressie held my hands. My brother Gedaliah, thirteen years old, held my father's hands. The doors were opened. Three Gestapo, wild with angry faces, pulled open the heavy doors.

There was no time to think. We were pushed, pulled. Orders were shouted in German to "form three groups, *shnell, shnell!*" The *shnell* was the most used German word of demanding to hurry up, *Mom explained as if I had never heard this word before. I remember this word very well. She used to touch my shoulder lightly and "shnell" me to prepare for school or to go to bed, and I hated these orders and those moments.*

Men on one side, and children and mothers on the other side. Young women in the middle. No confusion. No time to hesitate. Mothers were pushed with gun butts, and the children cried hysterically.

My father and my brother were forced into the men's group. They stood in a long line with other men and boys humiliated, defeated. They moved forward. I waved good-bye. This was the last time that I saw my father, the last memory of my father—my father, Meir, holding my brother Gedaliah's hand as they disappeared on the platform of the train station in Birkenau and recessed into a memory, a painful memory of hopelessness. I never saw them again.

My mother, my sister Blanca, and her children, little Judah and Ressie, were pushed toward the women and children's lines, and this too was the last time I saw them, the last memory of them. The Polish couple from Budapest was right. They told what happened to mothers and children. And we just did not want to believe.

My sisters Yocheved, Sorrah, Rassel, and I were pushed to the young women's group. Everything went fast. We did not have time to think or cry.

And years after the war, Mom still avoids traveling or getting close to a train station. "Trains bring bad memories," she whispered, managing to avoid trains at all cost even when it came to sending me, a seven-year-old, all by myself to visit my real father in Haifa. She taught me how to take a bus from Benie-Barak to the train station in Tel Aviv and never traveled with me, and I knew why.

SS guards walk along the arrival ramp at Auschwitz-Birkenau.
[Photograph #77220]

5

Birkenau

We were pushed into a line of young women, "healthy-looking" women, my sister's arm under my arm. We were holding each other tightly—inseparable. We feared separation. We were afraid to lose each other. We were the family now, two sisters alone in a broken world. I searched for my younger sisters Rassel and Sorrah but did not see them anymore. They were forced forward with guns toward the unknown, and they disappeared forever. We never saw Rassel and Sorrah again.

The Gestapo worked fast. They formed groups and lines and moved them forward, shouting, pushing, and kicking. It was impossible to resist, impossible to think or to feel, just fear and anguish everywhere. Mental confusion. We turned to lines of people, unfamiliar faces—no family . . . no sisters, chaos . . . the end . . . the beginning of the end.

We were grouped into rows of fives. *Mom's voice turns cold, rational. She speaks as if it was happening to somebody else, her unique way of distancing herself from the pain. And I wonder how she does it, telling the most difficult experiences without falling apart. She tells her story, and when finished, she leaves her room, joins her friends, the elderly in the nursing home, for the four o'clock tea and cake.*

We marched quickly following the Germans' "eiein, tzvie, drie" (one, two, three), moving fast toward the iron gate with a tall tower. We passed through the entrance and we saw a sign, Auschwitz II-Birkenau.

We marched silently, stifled by fear, preserving some energy for the unknown. There were lines of people marching on the right, on the left side, in front of us, and behind us. Lines of men, women, children, elderly, young, and old were all walking into the camp through to the gate.

The SS were holding dogs, German dogs, well-trained shepherds that did not bark but waited compliantly for their orders.

A giant German officer blocked our group. He had a scary-looking face, a round red face radiating hatred, rage. He was wearing black boots meticulously shining and held a terrifying dog. His first words to our group were, "You are now prisoners of the German army." *Mom remembered the exact words.* "You do exactly what we tell you to do, you obey. If you do not obey, you die," he yelled in German, and the capo, also a Jewish prisoner, translated the order to Hungarian and to Yiddish, the universal European Jewish language that we all spoke at home.

My sister and I understood the German order—we were fluent in German. It was our father who taught us the German language, which was unusual for a typical Jewish family. He believed that knowing languages can save our lives, and he was right. *Mom exhaled noisily.*

"You are now entering the gate of Birkenau, this is a German camp." The capo repeated, "Here in the camp, if you work hard, you live, if you do not work, you die. You must obey the orders." The German slogan was continuously reinforced, "You work hard, or you die, You cry, you die."

We entered the gate of Birkenau. Lines of desperate people, tired men, mothers holding crying babies on their arms, children carrying bags on their shoulders. Exhausted people. And Gestapo, SS, yelling, screaming, giving orders, rocking with their shining leather boots, *Mom remembered.*

The German boots, black shining boots that I was forbidden from wearing. I was not allowed to purchase any boots in my teens. Boots were forbidden in our house. Mom did not like them at all, and I knew why.

A mass grave in Bergen-Belsen concentration camp.
[Photograph #32072]

6

Auschwitz

The lines moved forward. There were three capos in charge. The Germans "delegated" authority to the capos. They were Polish Jews, prisoners themselves that had particular capabilities to rule, to control a group of prisoners. They had a patch sewed to their shoulder with the letter *J* for their Jewish identity. The Germans appointed the capos to control the prisoners, Jews managing their own fellow Jews.

Most capos were cold and distant, *Mom remembers,* and we were looking for some compassion, a little understanding. We were all Jewish after all destined to the same fate. But our shared similarity did not help. The capos were rough. They had to prove to the Germans their loyalty and to keep their favor so that they would not end up as the rest of us.

The capos had to act this way, *Mom justified and made herself clear.* They were prisoners too, most of them Polish women that were to Auschwitz three or four years prior to us the Hungarians. The German chose the toughest women and trained them to become more vicious, more efficient. The capos were held responsible for the prisoners. They had to perform as they were expected. And they could lose their "rank" and become a regular prisoner if they did not perform their job as expected.

The capos acted as the SS did, cruel and brutal, with the exceptions of the very few that preserved some humanity and found ways to help without getting in trouble.

Forty years passed by, and I can still feel the fear and the shame when our angry neighbor spitted into my face, blaming my Mom, saying, "Your mother was capo." I was ten years old but can still see his angry eyes, mad icy blue eyes, blaming and shaming my mother, saying she was capo and the things she did in the concentration camp—I did not believe him. He was crazy. We all knew that he was crazy from his time there. He witnessed the worst of all, the brutal murder of his wife and children. I did not talk about it, did not ask Mom, did not investigate, just absorbed the shame, and it was scary. I remember the humiliation, the fear, the confusion. And the mystery of it haunted us for years. I never had the courage to ask . . . and the hard feelings remained.

"You are not allowed to speak your language anymore, you communicate in German only! You are now entering Auschwitz!" the capos screamed. "This is the worst camp on earth, you will see your family burn to ashes, there are gas chambers and crematoriums, they burn day and night, and you will see and smell it, and if you are lucky, you work and get some food! If you work and obey you will live."

The capos prepared us for the worst of human experience. And we soon learned how right they were.

The walk from Birkenau to Auschwitz lasted several hours, *Mom remembered.* As soon as we approached the gate of Auschwitz, we knew that the capos were right. They did not exaggerate. We saw the barbed wire around the camp, the long rows of brick buildings, the watchtowers, the searchlights, the barking dogs, and the SS.

People were walking, standing, busy with tasks, or getting ready for something.

And the smell . . . the smell . . . burning flesh . . . and flames, gray flames thrown toward the sky, forming dark clouds . . . black and heavy clouds made of human ashes. We all looked toward the crematorium, saying nothing, not a word. *Mom's voice faded away, and I feel my own fear crawling into my heart, scared. I want her to continue. She never talked about the crematorium. She needs to continue, and I keep quiet. I want to hug her. I am thousands miles away. I can't find a word.*

"You see the flames . . . you see your family . . . your mothers, fathers, sisters, brothers, children . . ." the capo continues viciously, and I knew then at that moment that my family was gone. They were gone forever, *Mom says.* My sister and I were still alive, but the rest were gone with the flames.

I suggest a break, but Mom does not hear me and continues her story. We did not have time to think or feel. We had to keep going. The capos and the SS shouted, directed us to a round central yard in front of a long brick building.

We joined a long line of women. They were waiting for a medical examination. German doctors and officers were managing the line, standing on the top of the line, examining naked bodies. The capos, walking up and down the sides, shouted orders in German, "Take off your clothes!"

We took off all clothes, woman after woman, naked bodies with no exemptions. The line got shorter. Naked women . . . short, tall, heavy, skinny. We were surrounded by body parts, shame, and fear . . . one after another . . . we stepped forward toward the medical group.

The medical team . . . checking bodies . . . head to toe, asking questions, assigning bodies . . . to the left . . . to the right. *How did it feel to stand there naked? Was it cold? Was it embarrassing?* I want to hear more, *and Mom did not pause.*

There was no shame. No humiliation, *Mom continued*, we were standing naked, watching our clothes pile up on the ground: dresses, underwear, bras, socks, piles of female garments. We watched one another tired and numbed. Nothing mattered. We followed orders, waiting for our sentence.

We wanted to look healthy to make a good impression on to the doctors. Looking healthy meant continuing to live to be selected for work. I was worried about my sister's appearance. Her body looked healthy, and she was round enough to make good impression, but her face was pale, bloodless. I bit my finger deep until few drops of blood appeared. I spread it in between my fingers and massaged my sister's cheeks, right side, left side. I wanted her to look healthy. She was still colorless.

The line got shorter . . .

Our turn . . .

The doctor in charge, the infamous Mengele, was holding a long stick in his right hand, turning it, moving it from side to side. Pointing the stick to the right was a sign for an examined woman to move to the right line. Pointing the stick to the left sent a woman to the left line. We did not know which line was bad and which line was good. There were two options, life or death.

And later we learned that the left line was for slave labor, an inhuman existence, and the right line meant annihilation with flames in the gas chambers.

We were terrified. No one dared to make a sound. We moved forward. My sister stepped forward. Dr. Mengele observed her body. She was tall, slightly round, with beautiful long dark hair. Dr. Mengele asked her how old she was, and she said twenty-four. He pointed to the left.

I was shaking. I wanted to follow her to the left regardless of what the left line meant. I just wanted to be with my sister, for us never to be separated.

My turn.

I stepped forward.

I saw Dr. Mengele's icy blue eyes. They were cold, sharp, and emotionless. "How old are you?" he requested.

"Twenty-six," I responded.

"Occupation?" he continued.

"I am a road builder," I lied without thinking twice, trying to make strong impression. I knew that a road builder would have a better chance for survival.

He observed my body from head to toe, from side to side and signaled with his finger to turn. And I turned, slowly, naked, shaking. "Healthy." he nodded with his head to his team in German. *Mom remembers the exact word.* "Healthy," he said and pointed to the left. And my heart dropped down into a deep hole.

I moved fast toward the left line, standing behind my sister. To live or to die, it did not really matter anymore, *Mom repeats*, as long as I was with my sister. Life did not matter without her.

And . . . left meant life.

A Jewish woman walks towards the gas chambers with three young children after going through the selection process on the ramp at Auschwitz-Birkenau. [Photograph #77217]

7

Assembly Line

The capos threw blankets to cover the bodies. Each woman received a dark grayish blanket, big enough to cover the upper body and a little more. We walked forward, cold and shaking, tightening and stretching the cover over our bodies, curling deep into the dirty cloth with an unrecognized odor.

The SS blew the whistle and pointed his stick toward the next barrack. Stripped from all identity and naked, we marched toward the barrack. I watched my sister. She was miserable, falling apart. I touched her back, pushed lightly, and moved her along the stream of terrifying bodies.

We arrived into the barrack—a large "grooming" hall. It was managed by several Polish prisoners, Jews. They wore prisoners' clothes, black-and-white stripes with a letter *J* (Jew) sewn on the right shoulder. They held clippers and shaving razors. Their duty was to cut and shave prisoners' hair—women's hair, blond, dark curls, short hair, long hair—erasing the last identify of the individual as fast as possible.

Cut and shave.

Cut and shave.

No lice.

Clean heads.

We ran in a line, woman after woman, forming a path of human hair on the concrete floor, a carpet of Jewish hair—brown, blond, black—an unforgettable carpet. Naked women covered with blankets, bald and scared of what might come next.

A very efficient assembly line, *Mom sighs*, the Germans . . . they were very organized.

I hear Mom's fascination with the German efficiency, the German order, the good organization, and it is a mystery for me, Mom's admiration for order. How can she see any goodness in the Germans' order, the people that destroyed her life, her family, and nation? "Ordnung muss sien," (order must be), *Mom said.*

In my last visit to Israel I choose a German flight company that passes through a German airport in Frankfurt. I wanted and needed to see this efficiency. And I watched the Germans' order. I needed a glimpse into the order that Mom described. I searched for evidence, and Mom is right—the flight attendant, the services, the airport stores, all in order and efficient.

I looked at the Germans' faces, young and old people in particular, Mom's generation. I search for evidence, for clues. Were they there? Did they see the horror? I needed to see if I there was still evil in their eyes.

We watched each other. It was hard to recognize our former selves, hairless strange women. My sister Yocheved changed and looked so different, stripped from the beautiful brownish hair, stripped from the curls that rolled down her face. She looked fragile. I wanted to hug her to comfort her. It was impossible. We were surrounded by capos and SS. Compassion was not allowed.

We were herded to the next station, to the disinfectants and showers. The capos were screaming, shoving, and shnelling, hurrying the process.

Whispers of fear and dread pierced the cold air. "Showers," we had heard about "showers," the gas showers. But there was no time for fear. The capos pushed toward the disinfectant barrels. Hungarian prisoners wearing camp uniforms (striped dark gowns) were dipping long-handled brushes into the barrels, dipping the brushes into barrels then pulling them out covered with dark fluid, chlorine and Lysol, *Mom explained.* Woman after woman received a good brush head to toe with disinfectants.

It burned, and I did not allow myself to feel. We continued toward the showers covered with Lysol, my sister at my side, and that was all I cared—to die in a shower as long as my sister was at my side. My sister was trembling. She was not built strong as I was, *Mom repeated,* not strong. She was weak and exhausted. I wanted to protect her. She lost her balance, several times, and I straightened her back up again.

We jumped into the showers. A cold stream of real water flushed our dehydrated bodies. "It is real water!" we yelled, real water coming out from the long metal pipe hanging from the ceiling. It was not gas as we feared. We were going to survive.

We moved to the next station, to immunization.

Two nurses, Polish prisoners, standing at the top of the line, held syringes, emotionless. They refuse to engage in direct eye contact with patients-prisoners while inserting needles. They were making their injections into the bare unshielded arms. We received immunization against contagious diseases, *Mom laughed.* The Germans were scared of germs, scared of epidemics. They protected themselves, never touching prisoners with their bare hands. They used sticks, rubber cords, and guns.

We continued on to the next station.

Capos threw prisoners' gowns into the hands of the women walking down the line. We caught the gowns and pulled them over our bodies covering our backs with no time to measure or find a perfect fit. There were small women and large women treated all the same, one size fit all. We ran forward shnelled and shoved into the next station. We all looked alike—hairless, barefooted, desperate, covered with baggy striped dark gowns.

We were hurried and pushed to next station toward a large pile of shoes. Used, torn-apart shoes with a story to tell, *Mom sighed.*

Each woman received one pair of shoes and moved forward. There was no time to measure to choose the right size. You either got the right size or you did not. *Mom added,* we were not allowed to change, to exchange, or to find the right size. And we continued in the line, moving to the next station.

I lost sight of my sister, and I panicked. I stopped and looked back. My sister was struggling to keep pace with the group. She seemed weak, lost, and giving up. I knew that I would have to turn back to pull my beloved back to life. My heart was pounding faster. I wanted to protect her, and I did not want to lose her. We were not allowed to hinder the flow of the fast forward assembly line, and I knew the consequences of doing it. "Ordnung muss sien." Order must be, *Mom translated.*

The capo noticed my attempt to help my sister. Her eyes turned cold and evil and flashed with anger. I realized that the next move would be agonizing. I have seen the capo retaliate in a malicious tantrum. The capo reached into my sister's back and, in the split of a second, hit her with a stick, cutting her flesh brutally, slashing the skin open.

My sister fell to the ground, and I felt as if a cold knife was being inserted into my heart. I was not scared anymore. I pulled my sister up and shoved her back into line.

Mom paused, and I heard her deep moan.

"You saved your sister." I searched for the right comforting words.

"Yes. I saved her life," Mom agreed for the first time.

"I returned to Sighet to save my family. I could have remained safe and hid in Budapest, but my family was more important than my own life, and my sister's existence was precious, more valuable than anything else in my life at that time."

A sign on the electric fence in **Auschwitz**.

The sign reads, "Caution, danger."

Date: After Jan 1945
Locale: **Auschwitz**, [Upper Silesia] Poland; Birkenau; **Auschwitz** III; Monowitz; **Auschwitz** II
Credit: USHMM, courtesy of National Archives and Records Administration, College Park
Copyright: Public Domain

8

Block 13

We marched through barracks, through long lines of flat one-story gray army buildings. Each barrack had an entrance and an exit at each side of the building. Prisoners with heavy faces and emaciated bodies were walking in and out the entrances. People that looked so different only a few months earlier were forced to do slave labor as a part of the German plan. Their lives were not theirs anymore. Their only guilt was that they were Jewish, *Mom added.*

Women were gathering in groups at the front yards. They all looked alike—uniformed skeletons covered with striped gowns. Some heads were covered with a little hair, the hair that grew after the shaving. Others had kerchiefs. The married women, they kept the tradition to cover the head, *Mom said.*

They were holding shovels, the women. They were raking the ground, in pairs, shoving dirt into sacks. One woman was holding a paper sack and the other woman was shoving dirt directly into it, trying hard not to miss, to avoid trouble. They looked tired and exhausted, with no expression on their frozen faces, bending forward, performing tasks under the supervision of the SS with their terrifying dogs by their sides. The poor women didn't see us, a new human convoy entering the camp. Their minds were deep in their own thoughts to complete their tasks and survive.

I searched for a familiar face, for somebody that would have known anything about my family, maybe a relative, a neighbor from Sighet, but there was no time to look too much. The guards yelled and hurried the group to run. We walked faster and faster to keep up with the capos' pace.

We were exhausted and numb.

And then we felt the smell. *Mom inhaled deep into her lungs as if she was still smelling it.* A strange, heavy odor filled the air, a smell of a burned flesh. The air was filled with smoke, and it was a suffocating smell. Dark flames were thrown toward the sky through the chimneys on the top of the roof. The smoke was paralyzing. We were petrified.

We knew without saying a word the death odor. It was coming from the crematorium. The smell that constantly churned our stomachs floated in the air and gushed out of chimneys from the crematoriums, the death assembly lines.

The camp was naked, with no reminder of nature's beauty in the Polish countryside. There were no trees, no plants, only gray bricks, *Mom detailed.* There were only a few gray trees, lifeless and leafless, with a few dried branches decorating them. The human ashes and the smoke, *Mom remembered,* consumed the trees.

We arrived at our new "home," Block 13. It was a large gray building with two entrances at each side of the building. We passed through the first entrance. The space was filled with rows of beds. All the beds were connected to level, beds, bunks, from wall to wall. The beds were rough wood boards, two levels of stretchers, no mattresses, *Mom explained.*

We were shnelled into groups of fives.

The capos were anxious. They pushed and hurried us to get into the bunks, to get ready, to prepare for sleep for the first night in Block 13. We crawled into the nearest bunk on the first level, my sister at my side. I touched her arm lightly with no words, only our hearts beating faster and faster, happy to lie down. We curved into each other's bodies, connecting and relaxing the fear, the fatigue. Three more Hungarians crawled into our bunk. They were three sisters, the Wiseman sisters, our neighbors from Sighet, from the Serpent Street.

The capos threw blankets, one blanket for each bunk of five women. The covering was an army blanket or *kotz* for each bunk. It was not large enough for five women—it covered only three women, those in the middle.

We lay on our sides to fit in the small flat. The naked wood boards were rough, but it didn't matter. We were tired and fell into a deep sleep.

This was the first night in Auschwitz, a night filled with terrifying dreams. Nightmares . . . *Mom hesitated as if reliving her fleeting, recurrent dream.* The first night . . . the nightmare . . . we were captured in the wagon. Again, the last journey with my mother, father, sisters, brothers. We were piled up on the wagon floor, trampled under SS boots. We were smashed on the wagon floor, the SS energizing the vicious dogs, sending them into the line of the naked people that were waiting for showers . . . and the wagon with its quick wheels that rolled into flames.

Mom's dreams appeared again, emerging at nights, years and years after Auschwitz. Wild dreams, longing for her mother, father, sisters, and brothers reactivated her heartache and reawakened her sense of loss. Late at night, I used to hear Mom crying out in a bad dream, mourning quietly at night, deep in the dark, mumbling in a different language. We did not talk about those dreams. I knew that Mom was there again . . . in that horrible place about which I was not allowed to know or to ask.

The first morning in Auschwitz was impossible, *Mom continued the following day.* It was still dark outside when the capos burst into the block, yelling, awakening everybody, throwing hands to the right, to the left, giving only few seconds to organize for an *appal*, the routine German roll call. Our Jewish sergeants were screaming orders, to stand in lines in rows of five outside of the barrack at the front yard.

We ran to form the lines in rows of fives. We stood still for an hour, my beloved sister on my right side. We were forbidden from movement whatsoever. We stood, motionless, waiting for the SS, for the name call, for the numbers call, to check for a possible escape. The SS, accompanied with a scary dog, was walking in between the lines.

The dog, doing his task, stopped near a woman, thrust his nose into the wet ground, and discovered a crime. A woman, who was unable to hold her bladder, urinated on her self while standing in line, creating a small puddle in the dried sand. The dog did not bark. They trained the dogs not to bark, *Mom added.* The capo took charge. Her face flashed with anger, she hoisted her hand and flogged her stick into the woman's back. The woman collapsed on the ground. We froze with terror.

It was the first lesson in Auschwitz, *Mom moaned.* We were all horrified. I tightened my legs, shaking, using all muscles necessary to prevent an uncontrolled accident. We all needed to urinate, but we were not allowed to do so at that time. Using the bathroom was permitted only at a particular time such as after an appal or when the capo decided so.

A metal bowl filled with dark watery liquid, coffee, was given, and it was passed from hand to hand, from mouth to mouth. Each row of five women received a bowl. And we watched each mouth carefully, assuring a fair share of coffee.

The roll call ended, and we were allowed to go to bathroom in the backyard of Block 13. It was an outside bathroom made of a large hole that was covered with disgusting dark fluid. And there was a wood board that stretched from one side of the hole to the other, a dangling board that made it scary and difficult to concentrate. I was scared of falling into the mud of the human waste.

We were allowed to empty our bowels twice a day, only twice a day, *Mom repeated,* and there was always a long line of women waiting for their turn. Having to wait in line and the fear of falling into the mud caused constipation, changing our bodily functions, *Mom said.* And this was when I began to suffer from chronic constipation.

The chronic constipation was an uncomfortable ailment thrust upon Mom from the rigors of life in the concentration camps. She suffered from it after the war, and until this day, Mom drinks senna tea to improve her condition. I was only six years old when Mom taught me to prepare the "helping" tea, the senna tea.

Mom taught me the exact way to make the tea: take a handful of senna leaves and place it in a tea glass, then add a good boiled water, cover the glass with a small glass plate, and let it simmer for an hour or so until the water has a dark color, and that meant that the tea was strong enough. It had to be strong so it would help. Mom drank it slowly only after it got colder. She strained the leaves with her teeth, preventing the leaves from entering her mouth, drinking only the tea, and then spitting the leaves on the glass plate. It was bitter, but it helped. I did not understand her condition then. I just knew that this tea was helpful for "the problem" that had started in the war when Mom was in Auschwitz and could not go to bathroom when she really needed. And I had became a tea expert for my mom at the age of six.

I was not allowed to hear or to know more details because "children do not need to know." And when I asked Mom, she told me that I would learn about it in school, from books.

A loud whistle cut the air, and bathroom time was over. Most women were lucky to finish their tasks, but some missed their turn. We were rushed, hurried to another appal, and this one was an appal for an individual assignment to work. The capo called names, and we lined up for a march to work. We walked in rows of five toward the center of the camp.

The SS marched at the top of the line before the first row. Her face foretold danger. She held a long leather rod, hoisting it up and down, side to side, as if a wagoner rushing horses. My sister marched at my side along with the three Hungarian women from Block 13. We formed a row of five.

A whisper in Hungarian was suddenly heard. The SS turned her head backward. It was too much for her. She stopped and searched to find the source of the whisper to find who dared to whisper in a forbidden language.

The capo was intrigued. She took charge, looked at the women's faces, and found the poor woman that defied the rules to use only the German language. She was twenty years old, a young Hungarian woman that forget the rules to keep quiet while marching and to speak only in German. The capo pushed the woman aside directly to the hand of the enraged SS.

The young woman landed on the soil. The SS flogged her with the leather stick. Raising her hand up and landing it sharply on the woman's back, the SS strapped her flesh and ripped her gown. The poor woman was bleeding. Her body was shaking with each flog until the torture stopped and then the body was dragged aside. We continued to march devastated and brokenhearted.

View from atop the train of Jews lined up for selection on the ramp at
Auschwitz-Birkenau.

9

Life on the Verge of Death

We headed into the kitchen barrack. The SS were marching on the sides, yelling orders, shnelling the group. We followed the orders, shaking with fear, just hoping to survive. We stopped walking when the SS stopped, listened carefully, and paid close attention to the SS tempo to prevent more tantrums.

"Shnell" was Mom's favorite word to hurry me every morning to be ready for school. It was the first German word that I learned from my mother. She shnelled me with a light touch on my back and shoulder, and it felt so pleasant—my Mom's rare physical touch. She loved the German language, and I could not understand how it was possible to love anything German, anything related to the murderers. Even now, she still loves to read magazines in German. "The language is not to be blamed," she always said. "The language is innocent."

And when I fly to Israel to visit my Mom, I buy the Stern, the German magazine that I can find only in Frankfurt, at the airport. I buy it at the kiosk from the seller, a nice, polite young German that was born years after the war. When I purchased the magazine, I looked at his face wondering about his parents and grandparents. Where were they when my mother was in Auschwitz? Mom's vision is deteriorating, and she can hardly see the writing, but she still sees the pictures in the German magazine, and she loves it.

We followed orders.

The capo yelled his final order before heading to work, "Divide into groups of two!"

The command was "to clean the front yard of the kitchen in pairs of two." The kitchen structure was a large brick barrack with a wide entrance and an exit. We were divided into groups of two. One woman was holding a metal bucket, and the other woman was raking the dry soil. One woman was raking the ground, and another was pushing the metal bucket, collecting dirt with her fingers and placing it straight into the bucket. There was no talk and no rest, each woman absorbed into herself, into her fears.

The capo entertained herself with the leather scourge—the *korbatch* in German, *Mom explained*—hoisting it up and down as if she was a well-versed wagoner that inflicted fear on his horses, making them walk faster and ran faster, never hesitating to flog the slow, the exhausted.

My body was aching, and my feet were swollen, *Mom continued the following afternoon just where she finished the day before.* I pretended that I was perfect. I did not complain, and I worked as fast as I could, pretending as if I had a big interest in cleaning as if it was the most important task, just to spare a blow, to stay alive, and to shelter my sister's life.

The steady gush of flames, with ashes flying toward the sky, was constant reminder of what could have happened to us at any second.

We were hungry, starving for a real meal, aching for warm soup, fantasizing about Hungarian goulash, stuffed cabbage, chicken noodles soup, anything.

It was lunch. We were commanded to stand in line, in rows of five, to receive a meal: a small piece of dry bread and a bowl of potato soup, watery soup with traces of potatoes floating. We walked toward a distribution table, woman after woman, in the right German order. Two capos, Polish Jews, managed the distribution. Each row of five women received one loaf of bread and one bowl of soup. The first woman, the closest one to the capo, received a bowel of soup filled to the top. The second woman in the row received a loaf of bread. The woman with the bread sliced it delicately, measuring each piece to make it equal sizes. The measuring size was a half length of a finger.

The woman with the soup, passing the bowl carefully, took three sips and handed it to the next woman, passing the bowl hand to hand, mouth to mouth. It was hard to decide to sip or to dip, to drink the soup, or to dip the bread into the soup. The soup was made of potatoes cooked in water, thickened with flour, an economic way to feed as many as possible, *Mom specified.* We sat on the ground in rows of five passing the bowl, hand to hand, mouth to mouth, counting each lip movement, waiting for our turn with big hungry eyes, *Mom described. The phrase became her motto.* "Hungry, big eyes." *This was how she described me when I did not finish the food on my plate. I knew then what she meant even without explanation.*

A sharp whistle cut the air, interfering with the few quiet moments of eating, of resting. An order was thrown to the air. We jumped, fearing the worst. We were ordered to join another group, a group of cleaners on the other side of the camp.

It was a shocking, unpleasant surprise, *Mom said, and I felt her need to reveal aching feelings.* I recognized them immediately. There were the Gypsies, *Mom said.* We were heading toward a group of Gypsies, our neighbors from Sighet, the gypsies that mocked us, that took joy from watching us being humiliated when we were thrown out of our homes in the ghetto on Serpent Street. The same four women that were delightful to see our lives being destroyed just a few weeks ago as we began our involuntary journey to this foreign land were now here in Auschwitz suffering with us as well.

The Gypsies noticed us and did not give any sign of recognition. It was hard to ignore their misery, *Mom revealed. The feeling of humiliation from the Gypsies still insulting my mom, she retold the story, the story of the Gypsies' betrayal, over again, during the years. Despite many other painful experiences, the Gypsies' shame was still vivid in her mind and in her heart. They laughed when the Jews were kicked out of their lives, homes, and future, but none of the Gypsies were laughing now.*

The Gypsies were actually the first to be thrown to the flames, *Mom continued.* They were finished at the gas chambers just like the Jews. They were also included in the Germans' extermination plan.

We marched back to Block 13 in rows of five. "Just go on," I told myself, murmuring quietly, reducing my own anxiety with a mantra that kept me going through the path of near death.

We arrived in Block 13 and were given supper, a loaf of dry bread with a bowl of coffee, a warm dark liquid. We passed the bread, hand to hand, each woman cutting her little piece, slicing equal shares, accompanied with eyes watching carefully, measuring each piece. We ate small bites of bread, dipping few crumbs in the coffee, eating slowly, delaying the end.

We climbed into the bunk, the first level, exhausted and scared. My sister's body curved softly into mine, drifting, fainting into a world of dreams and nightmares.

We were sitting in the wagon—*Mom continued describing her dream*—and the children, little Ressie and Judah, were holding my hands. Yocheved was holding my upper arm. Father and mother were at my side. We were all together again . . . I loved those dreams . . . to be with my family once again, even in a dream to feel so close to them.

It was still dark outside when the capos entered the block yelling and cursing, hurrying us to jump out of the bunks, awakening everybody with their whistle-blowing. The capos rushed us hysterically, readying us for a roll call while the SS were watching the capos' performance, observing them from a close distance.

Roll call started at 5:00 a.m., exactly the German time. The capos themselves were threatened constantly to perform, to control everyone efficiently. Otherwise, they would lose their status and become prisoners just like us, *Mom explained. I tried to imagine the pressure, the fear that the capos endured, to imagine who among the people that I knew, acquaintances, friends, and neighbors, could have been capos.*

We were shaking and cold, frozen with anxiety, covered only with one thin layer of cloth, a thin layer, a prisoner's gown. The SS called names and numbers. Most women had numbers carved in their arms, tattooed on the right arm. In response to the call of a name or a number, a woman stepped forward to show her presence. My name was called, Rachel Moshkovitz, no number, only a name—I did not have a number carved in my arm.

I was always fascinated with Elena's arm. Elena was my mom's friend from Sighet. She was also a survivor from Auschwitz. She had a number carved on her right arm, a dark green number, tattooed and embedded deep in the flesh. I frequently wondered why my mother never had a number.

The SS voice was sharp, cold, and scary. The way they pronounced our names was strange, terrifying. The German accent was rough. We listened carefully, worried that we would not comprehend the pronunciation fast enough. A woman that did not jump forward quick enough was jeopardizing her life.

Morning roll call was long, a daily torture, to stand in the cold at dawn, to recognize the names through the German pronunciation. We stood in the cold listening for our names and the numbers and controlling the bladders, fearful of an accident. And accidents happened. Women urinated standing, small drips between their legs, uncontrollable involuntary body movements. The capos, attentive to every little puddle on the dry ground, were furious. Women that lost control of their bladder were punished, thrown to the ground, and usually beaten to death.

According to the German rules, we were allowed to use the toilet only after the morning appal. A long line of woman tried their best to maintain their humanity and dignity, waiting for their turn to clean up.

Using the toilet was a frightening experience, *she continued.* Stepping onto a dangling board and peeing into dirty mud was terrifying. It was difficult to concentrate, fearing a fall into human waste, human mud. My stomach was swollen from holding in the excrement.

After a few days in Auschwitz, we were permitted to walk in small groups independently to the kitchen barrack to receive bread and coffee at morning time to bring it to the front yard—the eating site of Block 13.

The little freedom turned into a dangerous game. We learned quickly the "jungle rules," *Mom reveals.* The veteran prisoners whizzed through the camp life, practicing a vicious game. They snatched food from the hands of the new prisoners, the inexperienced. The thieves would walk along our group from the kitchen to the block, and as soon as we were far enough from watchful eyes, they "incidentally" tackled a prisoner, snatching bread from the victim's hands.

It was shocking to learn that a fellow sister, a prisoner like us, enduring the same fate, acted like that. Those of us with more civility learned quickly how to defeat their plan. We consumed the bread as soon as we received it. The bread was safer inside our stomachs.

View of the execution wall next to Block 11 in the **Auschwitz** I camp after liberation.

Date: After Jan 29, 1945
Locale: **Auschwitz**, [Upper Silesia] Poland; Birkenau; **Auschwitz** III; Monowitz; **Auschwitz** II
Credit: USHMM, courtesy of National Archives and Records Administration, College Park
Copyright: Public Domain

10

First Friday Night

We returned back to Block 13. Our day had consisted of long hours of digging, shoving dirt, carving a ditch in the dry clay soil. *Mom stops to breathe deeply as if she is trying to regain her energy.* The order was to enlarge and deepen a ditch that harbored an electric wire, those wires that were meant to prevent escape, to alarm the soldiers in the control towers, an electric wire to prevent escape surrounded the camp. But it did not scare desperate prisoners. Some walked through the ditch into the barbed wire that fenced the camp and received a gunshot wound from the control tower, ending their misery.

We dug with shovels carefully, not knowing how the wiring was inserted, afraid of touching the electric cables in error. We had just completed our first week in Auschwitz, and anguish started to sink in.

It was the first Friday night in Auschwitz, the Sabbath. After a challenging week of following orders, days and nights, it all blended, days melted together. We were confused and hungry. The Polish capo reminded us that it was Friday, first Friday night in Auschwitz, far away from the family. Evening roll call was over, and we crawled into the bunks, lying on the bare wood, stretching the cover suitable for only three over five exhausted bodies.

A soft melody floated in the air. I recognized the Sabbath hymn in a beautiful soft, mesmerizing voice, "Shalom aleichem malachie hashalom." Gradually, the silence in the barrack was replaced by the Friday night Jewish song—shalom to the angels of Shabbat.

My heart dropped. I missed my father. Woman after woman joined the whispering, adding a soft light touch to Shabbat voice. I felt closer to my father. It was his song, a Jewish melody, a song of faithful men worshipping their God and blessing the angels of Sabbath—our angels of peace. I could feel my father's spirit encouraging me to continue.

They were Saturday nights, Mom, sometimes it seemed as if every Saturday night you would sit beside the big radio in the living room, listening to the cantor, and say, "He sings like my father." With tears rolling down your face, you would listen to the music and let your tears roll. I dried your face with a linen handkerchief, an ironed handkerchief that you brought from Germany after the war. I felt your longing, but you did not talk. I was dreading those moments, Sabbath nights near the radio, your pain, Mother, embedded in my childhood. And today, when I hear a cantor sing, I remember your deep sorrow, and the memories of your sorrow permeates in my heart, and that feeling makes me miss you and my family that I never had.

I could feel my father's spirit as we sang the Sabbath song. He was there momentarily in Block 13 in Auschwitz on Friday night with my sister and me. We did not talk, only hugged and whispered the song and drifted into sleep.

Sabbath morning was a regular workday in the camp. Roll call started at dawn, SS calling names and numbers, and a waiting line for the restroom soon followed. Afterward, we had breakfast as usual, which consisted of a dark watery coffee and a dry piece of bread dipped into the coffee. Next, we marched in fives to work site.

We were ordered to the men's side—men reside in a different area in the camp. Each woman received a shovel, a short-handed shovel.

The command was to dig a sanitation tunnel. Three SS monitored the performance. We worked fast as men, preventing punishment, keeping up with the men's pace. Any woman that got tired and stopped momentarily received blows. No back-stretching or rest was permitted. Once we finished the digging, we marched to the kitchen in compliance with the orders of the SS.

Along the way, we passed by a group of prisoners. They were standing in a line to receive food. A man in an elegant suit caught our attention. A man in an elegant suit in Auschwitz! He did not wear a uniform as the other prisoners did, and he looked familiar. We moved closer. I recognized him. Mr. Horthy, the head of the Hungarian government. Mr. Horthy, a loveable leader, was thrown out and forced out by the Fascists, the new government. It was unbelievable, a shocking surprise, to see Mr. Horthy in Auschwitz, *Mom overwrought.* His "crime," *Mom explained,* was allowing his son to marry a Jewish woman. The German punished him also for that.

Mr. Horthy was given a special privilege in Auschwitz. He was allowed to wear a suit, a distinguished look in a camp of prisoners. The Jewish community in Hungary liked Mr. Horthy, *Mom added, still troubled by Mr. Horthy's fate.* He was good to the Jews, *Mom emphasized.* He preserved the Jewish rights, respected their unique needs—their tradition. The Jews had faith in the Hungarian government. They believed that they would be protected. They hoped that the Hungarian would not allow the German invasion and that the Hungarian would not allow the extermination. But history proved otherwise.

There were other political prisoners in Mr. Horthy's line—Russians, Polish, and Hungarians. A cloth letter pinned on their shoulder marked them. The letter C for communists, the letter R for Russians, and the letter P for Polish.

This meeting was our first encounter with male prisoners, the first conversation with them. They looked healthier and benefited from better living condition.

The capos were busy. They talked to the capos that guarded the political prisoners. And we had a little freedom to talk, to converse with the men. A little piece of newspaper was passed to our group, a small piece of a real newspaper, smuggled into the camp by a Czechoslovakian prisoner. This was how we learned that the Germans were losing battles with the Russians—the Russians were advancing their forces, defeating the Germans. Allied forces were destroying German camps, railroads, and transportation. We stood in silence then cheered inwardly, speechless. Hearing the news was a dream that came true, a dream of getting a little knowledge and hope. The end was closer. The Russians are moving toward the Germans' lines, and the Allies were targeting and destroying Germans' bases. It was an injection of a new hope. And my beloved sister whispered, "Just go on," our helpful mantra.

A few weeks passed by.

Morning after morning, we were thrown out of our beds, brutally awakened for another day of horror, running to the front yard, forming rows of five, anticipating the worst. Women disappeared daily. Some vanished after they were beaten down for the smallest "mistake," and others disappeared after collapsing on the way to work or on the way back.

I saw the changes in my sister's body. The little fat tissues were already gone, melted away. Her body size got smaller and smaller. The small ends of her hair that had just started to grow had made her look different, so fragile. She could hardly walk. She struggled to keep the pace with the walking group, and most of the time, we did not talk, only stared at each other, understanding the need to save the energy.

I changed too. My body changed. My heart was numbed, *Mom groans*. The only thing that kept me alive was the love for my sister and the deep responsibility to keep her alive, to protect Yocheved.

It was already evening when we arrived in Block 13. We were exhausted, and we had to continue to the kitchen barrack. Yocheved was drained from marching with swollen feet. She could hardly continue. Her left ankle did not look well. From an early age, we knew that she was limited in her walking. She suffered from a congenital defect. She did not proceed to the kitchen barrack. As we passed Block 13, she sneaked into the barrack and climbed up to the bunk. She was hiding under the blanket, hoping that nobody would notice her missing.

The group adjourned toward the food line, a long line of exhausted women waiting to receive the evening meal, dry bread with watery coffee. Sometimes we received a little extra, a little margarine or jelly. I swallowed a little piece of the bread and stacked the other part in my shoe for my sister.

On the way back to Block 13, we were tackled by the Polish, the veteran prisoners, the hunters. They were waiting and hungry, ready to snag a piece of bread from starving prisoners, hungry women just like ourselves, *Mom concluded.*

And I feel her anguish, the disbelief in human nature, of what hunger can make people do. For you, Mother, food and human dignity was the most important value. "People should not become animals even when starving," you always said.

The hunters searched our hands and our bodies. They did not find even one little crumb. The bread was consumed, swallowed. I hid a little piece of bread deep inside my shoe that even the wild hunters could not find so that my sister could have a snack later.

My sister was asleep when we arrived at the block. Nobody discovered her absence, her sneaking into the barrack, and sleeping while we continued to the kitchen barrack. It was a pure miracle. I pulled up the small piece of bread and fed her. She could not chew. She was unable to swallow from exhaustion. She drifted again into the sleeping world. I touched her body lightly. She was breathing slowly, her skin feverish and wet. I cut the bread into small portions then softened it inside my mouth and ground it with my teeth, wetting it with my saliva. Then I inserted the bread into her mouth, small piece after another. She swallowed the tiny bits of pieces with closed eyes.

It was the fifth or the sixth week in the camp when we noticed a change, *Mom continued the following day. She always remembered in detail and continued her story at the exact point where she ended the day before.* Rumors were spreading in the camp. The Germans were defeated. Other camps were being destroyed. The Allies were bombing the Germans, and the rumors infused hope. The SS behaved as usual. They were dedicated, committed to their call, cruel and vicious more than before.

The weather was freezing and bitter cold, a typical European morning. We were summoned for to a special roll call. The SS were searching for qualified workers for a particular work project outside the camp. We stood in rows of five. The SS were walking in between the lines, searching each woman from the top down, surrounding each woman from the front and behind. Women that seemed qualified were ordered to step forward to join the long line of qualified workers. The rest, the ones not chosen, stayed in the camp to continue with the regular routine work, the cleaning and the digging.

Once again, *Mom moaned, and I could feel the relief and hear her sigh through the telephone from thousands miles away as Mom relived those moments.* My sister was also selected to join my group, the qualified workers. It was a miracle.

Jewish women and children who have been selected for death, walk in a line towards the gas chambers. [Photograph #77298]

11

Slave Workers

We marched toward the camp exit in rows of five, my sister at my side. I sensed her fragility. She was feeble and apathetic. Her frozen face worried me. "Just go on," I whispered. She did not hear me, and I continued humming Father's Sabbath song "Shalom Aliechem Malachie Hashalom," insisting on bringing her back to life to lift her vanishing spirit. There was a sudden change on her face, a glimpse of liveliness, a hope.

We walked through a path in between the barracks and turned toward a barbed wire that fenced the camp. The flames at the top of the crematorium continued to throw arms of gray ash toward the sky, an endless dark ash. We all noticed the flames and smelled the burned flesh but continued on to survive.

There were groups of prisoners, marching into and outside the camp, emaciated men, skeleton women, all covered with ragged striped camp uniforms. They were all skin and bones with gray faces and curved backs. We all looked the same, *Mom continued.* We saw ourselves in these people, a reflection of what we had become after weeks of hunger and desperation.

We marched outside through the gate of Auschwitz, the SS at our sides, carrying guns, dogs, yelling, speeding the pace. We walked for several hours until we arrived at the first destination. It was a train station where we were ordered to stop and sit on the ground.

A group of Polish contractors "welcomed" us. We were handed over to the supervision of the Polish. They were site managers that contracted with the Germans to rebuild the train station, *Mom explained.*

This transition promised a change, and optimistic feelings sneaked slowly into our hearts. We hoped for compassion, a little humanity from the Polish. They were local villagers contracted by the Germans to assist in rebuilding new railways. They seemed to be less intimidating.

A wagon loaded with gravel approached the station and stopped, making a loud shrieking noise. The two-sided iron door was pulled down to the sides, and its contents slid to the ground, forming a pile of little white stones.

The Polish contractors yelled orders in German, commanding us to fill the path in between the rails with the gravel and to spread it evenly, *Mom reflected, giving vivid details.*

We were divided into three groups. One group was given shovels, and another was handed metal buckets. The rest were using their bare hands. The women with shovels were ordered to fill the buckets with gravel, and the women with the buckets were instructed to carry them to the rails and empty the gravel into the space between the iron logs. The rest used their bare hands to fill the buckets with the little stones and carry the bucket to the rails, emptying its contents and spreading the stones in between the iron rails. It was a tiring work. Women that never before carried heavy buckets, never before built rail paths, learned quickly and even perfected their performance.

Within a few hours, our hands turned red, painfully red, with the skin cracked open and bleeding. We were hungry, depleted of energy. We had not eaten since we left the camp, and the Polish contractors did not show any signs of preparing food for us. They had to keep up with their contract to get the job done regardless of our hunger. We worked for several hours, and when we finished, we sat on the ground as we were commanded. My sister leaned over my back, and I rested my head on her shoulder.

We were shaken by a sudden noise. It was a locomotive rolling down toward the station, pulling with it an old army wagon. It was crawling slowly into the station and stopping. And to our surprise, we saw hands extending from the window, and in the hands, there were loaves of breads. Real bread was thrown toward us, bread from hands of people with smiling faces. It felt like a dream.

Everybody jumped. All women stood up and ran toward the wagon, to the window, as close as possible. They were jumping on top of one another. They were trying to catch a loaf of bread. Fighting. They hit one another, fighting for the bread. But I continued to sit. I was exhausted, unable to stand. My hands were swollen and bleeding, and my legs refused to move.

The locomotive driver, an old German soldier, looked at us, at my sister and me. His compassionate look promised to bring good fortune. He noticed our weakness, the difficulty of rising up and reaching out for a piece of bread. My sister sat on the ground along my side, worn-out. We were the only ones that did not participate in the fight for the breads. We were the only ones that continued to sit.

He noticed my attempt to stand and giving up to exhaustion. With a fierce move, he threw the loaf bread as far as he could, toward our side, just far enough for us to catch the bread. It was dark and black, a real country bread.

You retold this story many times over, and years after the war, it had become the motto of your life, a symbol of preserving human dignity even in a troubled time, in hunger, in cold, in suffering, and in particular when it comes to food. "People should keep their humanity even in hunger. People should not become animals, pigs," you always said. You continued to sit and did not want to become an animal, to jump on other starving women, for bread, and you received your portion.

Even in liberation, in Bergen-Belsen as your story unfolded, you did not eat all of the British food you were offered. You were careful not to gorge upon the soup with the little pieces of fat floating in it, the pork fat that "could kill a starving woman."

On the way back to camp, we shuffled through a dirt path and could hardly lift our legs. Our legs and hands felt heavier than ever, painfully heavier. We did not speak. We just glanced at each other, moving one leg after another, step after step, in the mud. We imagined the bunks. We missed the bunks, the wooden boards upon which we threw our bodies on, the cold pieces of wood upon which we stretched our aching bodies.

On the way back to the camp, we were transferred to the hands of the Germans, to the SS. They were as brutal as ever before, pushing the slow with their guns, their sticks, *Mom moans.*

My sister walked on the front row, and I walked right behind her. Those that walked in the front rows skipped the whippings, skipped the blows. The women that marched farther behind from the middle to the end of the convoy were beaten more often. They stumbled behind the weaker and received more beatings, often viewed as not being able to keep up with the walking pace. Just before we arrived to the camp, a woman fell to the ground after losing her balance. It was Miriam. We knew her from Sighet. She was a twenty-five-year-old young mother whose babies were taken from her arms and were sent along with other young children to the flames, to the gas chambers in Auschwitz.

Young children were killed immediately, *Mom explained.* They were not beneficial to the Germans. They were too young to assist with the war machine. They were sent to the flames, to the crematoriums. And from that moment, when her children were taken from Miriam's arms, she lost the spirit of life. She was half dead. She lost the will to live but continued to survive. She woke up each morning, worked hard, ate the small portions, slept on the naked wood flats. She was a good, caring friend like all of us in Block 13.

The SS officer did not hesitate. He pulled his gun and pointed it toward the ground, toward Miriam's body. She was still shaking. He ended her life with one bullet. Her body trembled for a few seconds. Blood squirted from her chest and flowed into the soil. The convoy proceeded forward, leaving Miriam's body behind.

The horror continued at night with the floods of dreams. The SS were chasing us. My sister and I were running for bread and running away holding the bread. My sister was falling, naked. We lay on the ground. Dogs were chasing us. The bread disappeared and fell over into the ditch, and SS were shooting in the air.

The following morning, we were awakened with screams, with blows. "We were too slow" in getting out of the bunks. The capos were outraged. They were constantly mad, even worse than the Germans, the SS.

We jumped out fast to the front yard for a morning roll call. It was dark and cold. We were ordered to line up in rows of five and to take our clothing off, to be naked for "selection."

The selection team included four "medical" prisoners, two SS guards, and a doctor that was a Czechoslovakian political prisoner. The team selected the healthier prisoners for a new field job.

My turn came. I stretched my back, straightened my body, and walked confidently forward.

I made a good impression.

The Czechoslovakian doctor checked my body. I saw his clear green eyes—they were good, and I felt that he was on my side. He looked at my body from the head to the toe. I turned to the right and to the left. My skin was clear. There were no scratches and no bruises. I had become thin. I had already lost the round shape of my hips and my little tummy that used to bulge had disappeared. My breast though smaller still looked good. I felt as the skin over my belly was hanging like an empty bag, but I put on a healthy posturing way.

"Spread your legs and turn around," the doctor ordered in German. And I felt a little compassion in his voice. It felt that he wanted to help, so I believed. I wanted to thank him but kept quiet. "To the right," the Slovakian ordered. I walked to the right line.

It was my sister's turn. She stepped forward stretching her arms from side to side. The doctor moved his head, pointing her to turn to the side. She turned from right to left slowly. The doctor signaled her to spread her legs. She opened her legs wide open. She looked so fragile from behind.

The doctor hesitated, looked at my sister longer. My heart dropped to my stomach. He signaled for more testing. She lifted her arms again, bent her right knee, stretched her left knee and turned again, following the Slovakian doctor's order. She passed at last and was ordered to the right just behind me. She joined the long line of "the healthiest." We were together again.

We proceeded to the gate, marching out of the camp feeling healthier and chosen. We marched toward the woods. It was far from the camp, *Mom said. She did not remember the exact distance but knew that it was far.*

We were heading toward the forest. There were many stories about the forests around the camp, stories about the military industries in the woods, stories about the manufacturing of deadly poisonous gas, weapons, and gunpowder.

It was early in the morning, and we were hungry. We started to feel the anguish, the fear of the unknown. The trees were green. They looked normal, tall, nurtured. There were faded shading leaves on the ground, and some fallen twigs, a real forest far away from gas chambers, flames, away from the ashes.

The forests provided a safe haven for the Germans, a place for industry hidden from the enemy and the eyes of the Allies. It was hidden from American airplanes that had already started to bomb the German military camps.

As we marched through the woods, unbelievable scenery unfolded. Rows of barracks, barrack after barrack, an amazing established military fort inside a forest, completely hidden by the innocent trees. We were ordered to stop at the third barrack.

We were handed into the supervision of a Polish contractor. He was a tall man dressed in a suit, a dark overused jacket and pants. One of those Polish foremen that contracted with the Germans, *Mom explained, adding historical fact.* He was a civilian contractor. The Polish man had very soft blue and tender eyes. They were promising, and we longed for compassion, for humanity. We craved goodness.

The SS gave orders to the foremen and moved aside. Blue Eyes took charge, leading the group into the barrack into a dark narrow corridor stuffed with boxes of gunpowder and bullet shells. The boxes were loaded along the sides of the walls.

We were commanded to form a group around a large table. Blue Eyes lifted a large box from the floor, pushed his hand into the first box, and pulled out a few empty bullet shells. He demonstrated to us a way to fill the shells with the gunpowder. His blue eyes changed as he was teaching the art. They turned darker and cold. His voice revealed imminent anger. "Each woman must fill at least two boxes within one hour," Blue Eyes warned. An impossible mission, *Mom added.* "And those that do not reach the goal will be punished," he said.

We were arranged in groups of five around rectangular tables. Blue Eyes pointed to the clock on the wall. The marathon had started.

We filled shells with gunpowder, shell after shell, scooping gunpowder with the left palm and pressing the powder in using a light force to tuck it in deep. There were no tools, only fingers. And the gunpowder had a dreadful odor. We inhaled the powdery stench. We swallowed the sickening odor. Our stomachs turned upside down with each breath.

We sat on stools and leaned over the tables, immersing ourselves into the fast pace. Some women succeeded in filling the shells fast. They moved finger after finger efficiently, filling deadly gunpowder into bullets. And others had trouble keeping up with the quick pace, and they struggled.

We filled bullets, counted bullets, counted boxes, watched the clock, measuring our future. I developed my own technique. *I heard pride in Mom's voice describing her system of moving*—finger after finger, filling, pressing, filling, and pressing. My pace was exact and quick.

My sister worked slowly. She was exhausted. Blue Eyes were watching. They got darker and scary. A reaction was coming. It was coming. An upcoming danger filled the air. I worried about my sister. What would happen if she could not make it, if she could not make at least two boxes in one hour? The foreman moved agitatedly in between the tables, his dark blue eyes radiating anger, blowing threats with unclear words, crazy words, some kind of mixed-up language of Polish and German. He walked as if an explosive bomb, searching for the exact moment, and the exact victim. He counted the boxes and counted those who did not reach his goal: two boxes filled with shells ready for the war machine.

Two women that did not reach the goal were selected for the show. They were ordered to step aside. His dark blue eyes exploded. He lifted his right hand as high as he could and swung the scourge frantically on the women's heads. His protruding dark blue eyes were filled with blood. "Eine, tzvie, drie." The madman continued the flogging up and down, up and down. I was frozen, distancing myself from that voice, from that terror. The two women collapsed. Their bodies were trembling, shaking, and shrinking as if minimizing contact with the scourge. Blood was splashed everywhere, on the wall, on the floor.

We had met the devil face to face.

Marching back to camp, nobody dared to say a word. We marched silently, shocked, each woman absorbed into herself, thinking of the brutal deaths of those innocent women and our own fragile existence. I longed for my family, for my stolen life, imagining my little bunk made of wood in Block 13 as if it was a little heaven. All I wanted to do was to hug my sister and to fall asleep in her arms.

We arrived at the camp exhausted and starving. We marched to the kitchen barrack. We were served the same regular meal that we received daily, a small portion of dry bread and a bowl of potato soup.

The soup consisted of warm water with a few flakes of potatoes in the bottom. It was finished within a few seconds. We climbed to the bunks. We did not see the poor women again.

The following day, we were heading to the forest again, directly to the gunpowder barrack, *Mom continued.* Each woman to the same seat from the day before. The task was known. We filled shells with the gunpowder and pressed the powder deep within the shell with our fingers, shell after shell, faster and faster. We feared the worst and tried to avoid the searching dark blue eyes. Nobody wanted to bump into the devil again. Our fingers continued to run, filling box after box, "helping" the German war. And his dark blue eyes were satisfied.

The gunpowder had a strong odor of poison. We did not know its danger then, nor did we have an option. Very soon, we started to feel its devastating effects. The chronic coughing was the first sign, *Mom sighed.* The gunpowder dust accumulated in our lungs, and within a few weeks, many women started to cough and spit blood and complained of aching bones, *Mom explained.*

We worked in the gunpowder barrack for several weeks. We walked to the woods early in the morning, filled shells as fast as possible, and then returned to the camp at dark. Upon our return, we would eat our bread and soup and then fall out exhausted on the bunks. The group got smaller. Several women became sick and disappeared. Some women did not get out of the bunks. They were unable to move and were taken to the recovery room. Others were removed to the crematoriums, and we did not see them again.

We were summoned to another selection. A team of three SS stood at the top of the line of the small group—the few that did not got too sick in block 13. The SS checked the emaciated bodies, pointing at those who would fit their needs for the new project. The first was told to step to the right side. She moved to the right, and several others behind followed her to the right line, anxious to know what was next.

Now it was my turn, *Mom paused, breathing a deep "ouy." She was keeping me in suspense as I wanted her to continue.* The SS pointed his finger. I stepped forward. The SS looked at my naked bones. There was no shame, no fear, no thinking, only a wish to continue living. I turned around, and they liked my bones. After a small consultation, I was assigned to the right. I was still worthwhile.

And then it was my sister's turn. She moved forward. Her hair started to grow out and fill the bony head. Her body looked as a skeleton. She lifted her bony arms up and then forward, following the SS's orders. She spread her legs to the sides, almost losing her balance! She was assigned to the left line. I was devastated and not ready to lose my sister, not yet. I could not see her face, but I imagined the worst of all.

We marched toward the gate, and to my surprise, my sister's group was marching parallel to my group. They marched toward the gate, and so did my group. I followed my sister with my eyes. She was placed in the second row. I recognized her round bony shoulders. My beloved sister, how much she had changed. We all had changed. We turned to "musleman." *Musleman, there was no need to explain this word. "We were all musleman," you used to say. We saw it in pictures, in books, at the Holocaust Days in school, that look of shaved skin and bones, walking in lines in the snow, in concentration camps. And this was how I knew, from the pictures, how you looked, and how your family looked on their way to the crematorium.*

We marched through the gate, to the woods, or so we believed, *Mom added. Her ability to pinpoint her thoughts and old fears is touching.* We were ordered to stop at a rail station. The site was a destroyed train station with broken rails. Broken bricks were scattered all over, and half of a wall was still standing erect as reminder of a building that served the station.

It was familiar work. We were well trained as experts were, *Mom laughed ironically.* We already knew how to line heavy rails, iron rails. We knew how to spread gravel in between iron bars, and to see this kind of work was a relief, *Mom continued, finding a little comfort in that time of horror.* I preferred to work in the open air, away from the deadly gunpowder.

My sister's group continued to the forest, to the gunpowder barrack. It was better for her, *Mom sighed, a deep sigh of longing for a sister as if she was reliving these moments again as if it happened yesterday.* My sister's health was deteriorating, and sitting on a chair and filling empty bullets was easier than working in the field.

A few weeks passed.

We marched to the forest day in, day out, two groups from Block 13—my group to the train station and my sister's group to the woods. Some stayed in the block, spreading bodies on bunks, half alive, half dead. We did not see them when we returned. Some joined the march to work and collapsed on the side of the road, dropped the ground and lay there, not even dead. Somehow, we were not even shocked, *Mom added.* We were numbed. We lost sensitivity. The only thing that mattered was surviving the next few hours, the rest of the day.

We were transferred into the hands of three soldiers, German women, simple soldiers, and low ranking, *Mom specified.* It was the first time to be under women soldiers. They taught us their way of laying the rails, their way of spreading the gravel and filling gravel between the rails. It was different from the way we worked with the Polish contractors. We carried the gravel in shovel and spread the gravels with our hands while standing in between the rails. We were divided into two groups. One group carried the iron bars, placed them on the ground, and connected them. The other group carried the gravel and spread them evenly with their hands.

We worked for hours until we were told to ready ourselves for a meal. We sat on the rails swallowing small pieces of bread, bite after bite, dark German bread dipped in dark coffee with the soldiers standing aside and watching us eating. One of them wore army socks made of gray wool. The left sock had a hole that was followed with running eyes all down the leg. It caught my attention, *Mom accentuated,* and I wanted to offer my help to stitch the hole, to catch the running eyes because I knew how to do it because it was my expertise. I was the family expert in sewing holes in socks. But it was too dangerous to offer, to talk to a soldier. She was too close to the other two soldiers.

The meal was over. We returned to the shovels, to the pile of gravel, to repair a German rail station. The officer with the ragged sock was getting closer to my side, and I whispered in German, "I can stitch the hole in your socks." She looked at my face and turned her head from side to side, looking to see if somebody heard it. But nobody heard it. I continued whispering, "Cross-stitching is my real profession," surprising even myself, *Mom admitted.*

The German seemed amazed. Was she surprised to hear my German accent, or was it my courage that stunned her? A prisoner who dared to offer help? To talk to a German soldier?

She nodded her head softly as if agreeing to my offer. I learned later that the German thought that I was a German Jew. I never corrected her impression. The German soldiers treated the German Jews better than the other prisoners, *Mom revealed proudly with her knowledge of the German language.* I thanked my father for teaching me German. He always said, "Speaking German could save a life." He was right. It saved mine in more than one occasion. My father was a unique melamed who taught not only Hebrew but also German, *Mom reminded me.*

The following day, at break, the German approached me while I was sitting to eat. I purposely sat apart from the group. She signaled with her eyes to step aside. I was shaking, fearful at what she was planning. I moved aside. She held my arm, moved it behind my back, leading, walking me toward the forest. I was terrified, fearful that it was the end of it all. How dare I offer her a deal? A Jew? A prisoner?

My arms were folded behind me in the German's hands. My legs kept walking toward the forest. We stepped inside the forest onto a small path that was covered with dry leaves.

The German ordered me to sit.

I went down and sat on a small rock. She unzipped her jacket and pulled out a paper bag. She opened it. There were three pairs of socks, threads, a needle, and a small chunk of bread. She handed me the small piece of bread first. She stared at my face to see my reaction. I lowered my eyes, scared, avoiding unnecessary tension. She handed me the socks, the needle, and a coil of threads, and then ordered me to repair the socks. Adding clear direction, she said, "You stay in the forest until I return you to the work site." In a case of an emergency, or a dangerous situation, she warned, "You run quick outside when you hear a whistle, and this will be the sign of the arrival a high-ranking officer."

A shiver crawled through my spine, *Mom remembered.* I sat on a stone surrounded with trees, isolated from evil. The ground was covered with foliage, with little fallen twigs. I was surrounded by real nature, and it felt as touching life again. I felt as if free, a real free woman.

I cut the bread into several pieces and inserted the larger piece inside the gown, keeping it for my beloved sister. The bread tasted as heaven. It was a German bread, a country dark bread, different from the one that we were given. With every bite there was a mix of joy and fear, a bite of bread and a slice of danger.

After inserting the thread through the little needle hole, weaving stitch after stitch, line after line, I felt as if I was living again, sewing my loveable stitches. The three ragged pairs of socks were now perfectly patched.

I sat on ground, stretching my legs on the sand, and rolling my head on the stone. *Mom paused,* dreaming about life in another world, imagining my family until a sharp whistle cut the air.

I jumped, picked up the bag, and ran outside as fast as I could. The German was waiting for me. It was not a dangerous situation, only that it was time to return to camp. I handed the bag to the German, and she put it under her jacket.

I felt my sister's bread inside my gown all the way back to the camp. I surprised my sister with a piece of delicious bread when we stretched on the bunk, preparing for sleep.

12

Stealing Bread

It was the fall of 1944.

The nights got longer, and the days got shorter. The capo distributed new clothing, new gowns to fit the colder weather. It was a striped gown, a little thicker than the one that we had before, to keep us warm in the freezing weather to come.

We received new shoes also. Shoes that were transferred from dead prisoners. They did not need shoes anymore. Their bodies gone, burned in the crematorium, *Mom detailed,* shoes became available in various sizes. We were not allowed to exchange shoes among us, but we did it anyway at dark, quietly and methodically. We would sit on the bunks just before preparing for sleep, and hands would move shoes from foot to foot. Some were lucky to find shoes that fit. Others had to cut the top of the shoe to make space for toes. My sister and I were lucky. We had shoes two sizes larger, brown heavy shoes that walked with us until the end.

Women continued to die. They died in stages. At first they were losing fat, layer after layer, then the muscles. The muscles deteriorated over time. Women were changing, transforming into skeletons. Many looked as if walking bones covered with skin. Others died on the side ways on the march to work or when returning from work, collapsing on dirt roads, left alone for nature to take its course. And others did not wake up from the night's sleep. Their bodies were removed to the fire in the ditches in camp after we left the block to work.

We lost our female cycle, the monthly reminder of womanhood. The Germans medicated the women. It was in the food. The Germans put in the food the medication to prevent the monthly bleeding because it did not fit the camp life as it could interfere with the performance, *Mom repeated.* They put the medication in the food, and we did not know it, nor that it would have mattered.

Food was the main issue of life in camp. We dreamed about food, talked about food, remembered the smell of home cooking, the mothers cooking at home. We cooked food in our mind, quietly sometimes and loud others, but always with a vivid imagination. Food became our major life theme, the main subject of discussion, an obsession. When you are hungry like that, your mind craves food, food, food, *Mom repeated,* and it will do everything to fulfill the desire.

We exchanged recipes of our favorite Hungarian dishes. When we rested on the ground for the morning break, we cooked stuffed cabbage. We took turns, woman after woman, cooking with words, whispering the process of cooking, the stages of cooking. We listened to one another quietly as we each described the process.

My turn to cook, I chose stuffed cabbage. I started with choosing the best green cabbage. It had to be light not heavy, and it had to have green leaves. To separate the leaves carefully, you boil water in a large pot and dampen the cabbage. You let the cabbage boil for few minutes until the leaves are soften. Then carefully fill the softened leaves, filling each leaf with rice mixed with ground meat, ground turkey, or chicken, or beef, with spices, Hungarian paprika, black pepper, salt, chopped onion. Fold and roll each leaf in an envelope shape, putting each stuffed leaf in a wide cooking pot so that each stuffed leaf will have a direct contact with the bottom of the pot for a nice crispy color and taste. Then after an hour of cooking, you add tomato sauce, a real homemade tomato sauce, *Mom emphasized. And years later, she kept teaching me, warning me, to always use real tomatoes for the tomato sauce. It was Mom's secret for a good stuffed cabbage.*

We listened quietly to the cooking of one another, one woman cooking with words and the rest listening and indulging in stuffed cabbage in our mind. The imaginary cooking and eating was giving a momentary relief, an escape from the constant hunger.

Another woman cooked chicken soup, and latkes—potato pancakes. The soup was warming our bones, and the latkes were comforting.

Each woman chose her own expertise of cooking and delivered her performance with many details as if it was a sacred ritual.

A sharp whistle cut the air. The break was over, and the "feast" was interrupted. We jumped on our feet and continued to spread the gravels with empty stomachs. The "cooking" continued at night as we stretched on the bunks and listened to more recipes being cooked in our minds.

My sister's health was deteriorating. She was hospitalized in the sick room for few days until she regained a little strength. Sick women were sent to recover in the sick room. Some were sent back to the block after regaining strength, but the ones that did not recover fast were sent to the crematorium.

There were days that we stayed in camp to do cleaning work, and those days were considered good days, much easier days. During those days, I worked alongside my sister and helped her in any way possible, especially carrying buckets of stones, bricks, dirt. I hid extra pieces of bread and fed my sister.

We were all aware of the German plan for *Vernichtung durch Arbeit,* Killing Jews with slave work, of annihilation through work and starvation, *Mom remembered.*

We were sent to the main kitchen, my sister and I and several other prisoners from Block 13. To work in the kitchen was a favorite job. It infused hope to be closer to food, to the big pots of soups, to potatoes, to breads. Prisoners from different nationalities managed the kitchen—political prisoners, Jewish prisoners, Polish, Hungarians, Romanians, and Germans.

I joined the Polish, my sister at my side. The Polish worked in the kitchen for several months. They knew the German rules for cleaning the kitchen all too well. We started with cleaning a large wood table. It was a cooking table, and we scrubbed with brushes, washed with water, dried with rags, shined, all in the German way. A smell of boiled potato soup transfused the air and made us dizzy, hungry.

We brushed another table, gazing at the stoves with big pots of soup boiling on top of the flames. We searched the shelves. They were covered with carton boxes filled with breads. So many bread in the boxes, and our stomachs ached with hunger, painful empty stomachs.

We stood in line for food. Big pots of potato soup were placed on a large wooden table. Polish prisoners were in charge of the soup distribution. The prisoners stood in line, slowly walking forward to receive soup in a metal bowl with a small chunk of dried bread on the side. Prisoner after prisoner walked forward with a painful hunger to receive the sacred meal. After receiving the food, they sat on the ground on the side, drinking the soup from the bowl and dipping the dried bread into the soup, piece after piece.

We had a few minutes to sit before returning to the barrack. We were getting back into a line, preparing to march. And I turned back to the kitchen, walking as fast as possible without drawing too much attention. I went strait to the bread shelves. I looked around—nobody noticed my entrance. There were five loaves of bread in a wood box. I snatched one, flattened it as much as I could, squashed it and hid it inside my gown under my breast. My heart was pumping blood at a tremendous speed, almost exploding. My legs were shaking. I walked outside the kitchen fast, my hand touching the bread, flattening it, making sure it did not show. I joined the line. Nobody noticed my move. My sister saw my quick turn into the kitchen and was relieved to see me returning to the line. The line moved forward.

A sharp siren cut the air.

The kitchen manager noticed the missing bread and notified the SS. The SS turned ballistic. They knew that the bread was taken by one of us. We were standing close to the kitchen barrack. The SS, along with the capos, started to search the women. We were directed to march to the kitchen backyard to take a distance from the crowd to ease the search process.

I knew that the end was coming. To steal bread was a major crime, and the punishment was deadly. The line started to adjourn, and I leaped aside and moved fast toward the line next to us. They marched slowly to the gate, leaving the camp to work at the forest. The prisoners were exhausted, indifferent. They did not bother noticing the new woman that just joined their line. I held the bread tightly pressed under my breast, flattening it to the bare skin. I walked as if I was always a part of this group. The SS with the dogs were looking for the prisoner with the stolen bread, sniffing, shouting orders. We left the camp, leaving the chaos behind. When we arrived in the forest, I departed and hid behind a tree. *Mom's voice is fading away as if she was relieving those fearful moments again.*

I sat on the ground for hours, breathless, fearing the worst. I continued to hear the dog barks, the sirens, and the shouts. At dark, I returned back to the camp and joined a walking group that passed by the woods.

The search for the missing bread continued for several hours. The SS did not notice that I was missing. My sister was certain that I got caught and started to mourn. The punishment for stealing food was particularly cruel, a deadly beating or, in the easier case, a fast shot in the head.

My sister was thrilled to see me back alive. She did not ask for details. I climbed to the bunk, cut the bread into four pieces, and split it with my sister and the three women on the bunk. The bread tasted as heaven.

Several weeks passed by. The weather got colder. It was a freezing European fall, something around September, October, or November. *Mom was not sure.* It snowed, and we were naked. We were wearing only winter gowns, and some were lucky to have blankets as an extra cover.

Winds of rumors were spreading in camp: the Germans were losing battles, but that information did not seem reliable. We did not see any signs of defeat. The SS were as vigorous as usual; the capo set forth orders, and we continued to work, to starve, to die, to get sicker, to lose friends, and to mourn.

People were desperate for news, for a little piece of the newspaper, for hints from the guards. Every little piece of news contributed to a small hope. The "rumor specialists" talked about coalitions, about the Allies, about the British and the American forces and the Russian army. The "specialists" revealed news from the front lines, described the bombing of the Germany and the damages to the German railways. They bragged about destruction of German bases.

But for us, it was a fantasy. We did not see and did not hear any wind of war, of defeat. We did not see any of it in the camp of Auschwitz. There was no sign of the end of our suffering.

A few weeks later, on an early Sunday morning, we were summoned for an unusual appal, roll call. We were commanded to gather in the front yard of the barrack.

The order hurried us "to pack all belongings, to put blankets on the shoulders, and to get ready for a long march." Fear and hope sneaked into our hearts, a fear of the unknown and confusion.

We had only a few minutes to organize. I helped my sister. She was shaking, consumed with fright. There was no talking, only facial expression that revealed the fear: we are leaving the camp forever, and our life is changing now.

We packed fast since there were very few belongings, just ragged gowns and blankets. We stood in rows of five at the front yard of Barrack 13.

Four young SS were heading the convoy. They marched at the top, and two capos walked on the sides. We marched in rows of five, not knowing the destination. Rumors were spreading fast: "evacuation of Auschwitz."

My sister walked at my side. We were watching each other, stepping carefully, silently. It was too dangerous to talk.

We marched under the iron gate, under a curved sign that said *Arbeit macht frei*—work brings freedom. We merged into a group of Polish prisoners.

We walked silently. We knew that we were leaving Auschwitz forever. *Mom paused. She was tired, and I heard the anguish in her voice even from thousands of miles away. I wanted to comfort her, to hug her, but she was so far away, and I could not reach her.*

We arrived at a Polish village that was occupied by the Germans, *Mom continued the following day.* Villagers were standing on the roadsides, entertained by the passage of a human convoy, watching the emaciated bodies of the Jews. Children were running back and forth, unaware of the real human tragedy. Bystanders removed hats, bowed heads in respect for the SS with their impressive shiny boots. We crossed through farms and passed by small houses with chickens strolling in the yards and cats and barking dogs. We passed by Polish children, blonds and innocent, with Polish mothers holding babies. We walked by elderly men sitting on small wooden chairs in front yards watching the Jews. For them, life looked normal.

We marched through dirt roads, passing villages, brushing with, almost touching, normal life. It felt as if we were breathing some normal life, seeing free people, seeing children playing in yards with cats, dogs, and chickens, women hanging clothes on metal wires, and an elderly chatting about the day's events.

We stopped at dark, dividing into groups and preparing to sleep in a barn. It was a barn close to a farmhouse, *Mom remembered so vividly.* The capo gave orders, forbidding us from making any contact with villagers. The barn floor was covered with dry straws, which was used for cow food.

A group of children followed us from a distance, fascinated with the SS guns and curious to see the walking skeletons. We looked at the children. It was painful, all the thoughts about the children in our family, my nieces, nephews that were gone.

We rested on a sidewalk of a house. An elderly woman opened the back door and stepped into the yard, holding a small pitcher of milk in her hands. She poured the milk—the precious white gold—into a small bowl and served it to the cat. We watched the cat, astonished. We envied the fortunate cat as it was lapping his milk up with his tongue and lips. We swallowed that milk in our minds. We craved that milk for our deprived and hungry bodies.

Envying a cat, *Mom repeated,* only a hungry person can envy a cat—*a moral wisdom you instilled into my heart many times over the years. And I learned from you how a person could feel when hunger strikes. I always had to finish the food on my plate because "food should not be wasted, and people in the war starved to death."*

The meal that we received consisted of a dry piece of bread with a little coffee, which was a dark watery fluid. We slept on the straw exhausted and drifted quickly into sleep.

We were awakened by a sudden noise. Heavy steps sounded on the roof. We anticipated the worst. A female voice whispered, "Shshsh . . . keep quiet, shshsh, do not make any noise, I have food, cabbage soup, fresh bread, for you. I lay it on the roof, and you take it after I leave."

And this was what we did. *Mom relived that miracle, the action of humanity.* I waited few a minutes for the steps to disappear and climbed up to the roof on a wooden ladder. I picked the bucket that was filled with soup, a cabbage soup—*Mom hesitated for a moment as if she was trying to be exact when telling the correct kind of soup*—and a large loaf of bread, white and fresh, that smelled as heaven. I held the bucket with two hands very carefully as a mother holding a fragile baby and stepped down.

The bucket with the soup was transferred from hand to hand, from mouth to mouth. We watched each swallow carefully, counting the exact number of sips each woman had taken, each lip movement. Each woman had three swallows and three little pieces of bread. We felt as if we finally made it to heaven.

The march continued on the following day. We walked through villages, railways, army camps, and German bases. And it snowed. We were wearing only a few layers of clothes. The luckiest had blankets to warm their bodies. We walked on a frozen ground, dashing through melted snow puddles.

We survived on two feedings a day: a piece of dry bread, a bowl of soup, and a few cups of coffee. We were hungry and starving with empty stomachs. Several women fell on the side of the roads as if dried leaves falling from trees. They were left on the ground for nature to take its course. The SS would sometimes rush the course by simply shooting the women straight to head to end their body convulsions. We just continued to march without turning our heads, without looking death in its face. We did not mourn the dead, the loss of a human fellow. We just kept going, each woman immersed in her own thoughts.

We walked shoulder to shoulder, watching one another's steps. My sister's foot was swollen, and she could hardly walk. She barely kept up with the group's pace.

Deep sighs interrupted the story. I felt her pain, which transcended the line and space even though we were talking over the phone thousand of miles apart. I could feel Mom's heavy breathing.

I held her arm, pulled her gently. The SS continued to yell and to strike the slow ones with their rifle butts. My sister and I continued along trudgingdodsing.

We walked thirty-five kilometers a day for six weeks, day after day, *Mom remembered,* sleeping in barns. Sometimes we were fortunate to get extra food from courageous villagers. An extra piece of bread, a dry piece of cheese, a little homemade butter, some tea, or soup would be terrific.

The SS slept in the villagers' houses. They occupied the houses and evacuated the families. The locals did not resist, could not resist. Otherwise they would have been shot.

13

Christianstadt

After long weeks of marching in deep snow, we arrived in Christianstadt, completely exhausted and sick. This labor camp was in the southern part of Poland, about eighty kilometers away from the Polish-German border.

The camp was similar to Auschwitz. It was one of the satellite camps of Gross-Rosen (Rogoznica), *Mom clarified.*

Brick barracks lined each side of the center. Prisoners were walking in groups marching in the center of the camp, busying with orders. The men's barracks were on the right side, and women's barracks on the left, and in the center were the administration barracks.

I felt a sense of relief when I saw the structured camp, a feeling of impending comfort, *Mom added, and I could imagine the feelings of "comfort" that she felt in the hell of this concentration camp.*

The barracks were organized in a meticulous order, in the German order, and it provided a sense of ease just to imagine the bunks inside, the possibility of sleeping and resting on the pieces of woods after weeks of walking in the snow and sleeping in barns.

The living conditions in the Christianstadt were somewhat normal at the beginning. There were no crematoriums, no gas chambers, and no human ashes thrown in flames to the sky. Only barracks, prisoners, SS, and work, work, work. We were reminded repeatedly that working hard would save our lives. A slogan was inscribed on a wall, *Arbeit macht frei*—work for the Germans, and you will stay alive.

People died from hunger, exhaustion, and hard work just as the Germans planned "Vernichtung durch Arbeit," annihilation through hard work and starvation, minimal food, harsh conditions, and slave labor.

We slept on bunks, my sister on my side, along with two Hungarian women Leah and Hannah, Hungarians from Sighet. We worked in workshops hidden in the woods. We were summoned to appals, the familiar roll calls three times a day, and we were divided into groups. Sometimes we were given options to work in a workshop in a building or to work in the field rebuilding railroads and paving dirt roads. I always chose fieldwork in order to obtain fresh air, but my sister chose to work in the workshop where she could sit and rest her swollen foot.

My sister stuffed gunpowder into empty shells, making bullets—it was a familiar job already. She sat on a chair most of the day and in a very primitive way with her bare hands and fingers stuffed gunpowder into bullets. After several weeks of touching and inhaling the toxic powder, the coughing started. She coughed badly and spitted blood. She became weaker and weaker.

Each morning started with yelling and shnelling, with the capos hurrying us to prepare for appal. They struggled too, the capos. They needed to preserve their fragile status to be in charge and in control. The first meal was after the morning appal. It consisted of dark watery coffee and a small piece of bread. We ate outside in the freezing cold air while we were given the assignment for the day. The SS yelled names and numbers. Most women had a number curved on their arms, *Mom explained. And I never understood why you did not have a number on your arm. All your friends had a number, but you never gave me any explanation. And to this day, I do not know the reason.*

It was an early morning appal when the SS discovered that there were two missing women. The SS yelled their names and yelled again even louder, two names, and there was no response. The capo was furious. It was her responsibility to get the prisoners ready on time before the arrival of the SS. The capo, a Jewish prisoner from Poland, ran back to the barrack, and she found the two frozen bodies. They died at night in their sleep.

It was not an unusual event when women died, during the day, during night, on the way to work, and back from work. And when a woman died, nobody made any move, and there was no sound or a tear of sorrow. We became indifferent human beings with no second thoughts and very little feelings, focusing on the present. Each woman controlled her own fears, focusing all thoughts around the next piece of bread, the next serving of soup, a cup of coffee, and breathing.

We were commanded to march. We walked toward the train station that was located several kilometers from the camp, and there we were divided. My group turned to the train station and my sister's group continued to the workshop in the forest.

Hills of gravel were waiting for us. As experienced women, we loaded the gravel into buckets and carried them to the wagon. We formed an assembly line of women, skin and bones, transferring buckets, hand to hand, arm to arm. An assembly line, *Mom repeated.*

There was a division of work—some loaded buckets, others transferred buckets to the next station, and the last group in the assembly line emptied the buckets into the wagon.

We finished the hill of gravel at dusk, straightened it completely, filling the wagon with small pieces of gravel. We left exhausted and hungry, marching back to camp.

We stood in line for supper to receive the regular portion of food when we heard a sharp blow cutting the air. It was a scary sound of a leather scourge landing on real flesh and blood. A furious SS hoisted a scourge up and down on a woman's back. The poor woman dared to receive two pieces of bread by mistake. The SS hit the emaciated woman until she crushed on the ground. The SS's face was red as if she was going to explode.

We stood quietly, silent, keeping our mouths shut. The poor woman tried to regain her strength to stand again, but she was unable to do it.

The capos assisted her and removed her to the barrack.

Her punishment was to sit day and night on a chair and dump her feet in a bucket of frozen water. She was so ashamed. We saw tears dropping into the bucket. She lowered her eyes, and I whispered to her a loving prayer. She had nothing to be ashamed of. We knew that. She was hungry, just as all of us were.

Rumors about the Germans' defeat and desertion of concentration camps started to spread. People talked about evacuation and burning of camps, about destruction of evidences of the German evil. The rumors helped to continue breathing, to sing as hope of surviving the hell. Every little bit of news triggered thoughts about home, about family and parents.

New deportees that were evacuated from Auschwitz revealed the new details: the Nazis were retreating and abandoning concentration camps.

The Germans evacuated Auschwitz.

And soon, we were on the run again, on the run out of Christianstadt. On an early Sunday morning, we were ordered to get ready for a roll call. There was something different in that roll call. The front yard was crowded with many SS, and soldiers were armed with guns and pistols. It looked as if we were about to leave the camp without returning.

Each woman received a small chunk of bread and was directed not to eat it. We were warned to hold it for dinner at that night. And it was difficult to keep the piece of bread for later, impossible to resist the temptation to swallow the chunk of bread all at once. We were all on the verge of starvation, but the fear of punishment for eating was stronger than the chronic aching hunger.

The SS yelled, giving us an order to start the march. It was a snowy, freezing day. All roads were covered with snow and small muddy puddles. Small flakes of snow landed on our bended backs. Agonizing with hunger and our spirit broken, we moved forward. It was this inhuman march that killed many. It killed those who could not survive the freezing weather and the hunger.

14

Death March

We marched in rows of five. The German meticulous order was kept all the way through, and it never ceased. We became accustomed to lifting the right foot along with the left arm and left foot with the right arm as if it was the law of survival. You keep going, or you die.

The SS on the top of the line was tall and heavy, a typical rough German army man. He walked fast, throwing his left boot forward followed by its right twin boot. We had to follow his pace. The Germans were on the run to leave the camp, but it did not interfere with the marching order.

The tall SS shouted orders, and the other two pushed those that could not walk fast enough. They pushed the slower with gun butts and beat the weaker ones.

We helped each other. My sister leaned over my arm, unable to walk straight. Most of us suffered terrible foot sores. It was only a miracle that we were able to continue walking. The cold wind hit our faces, and snowflakes landed on our shoulders. We slowed down. It was impossible to continue with the giant's pace. The SS could not believe our dare. He lifted his scourge up and down to increase the walking pace.

The first victim was a young woman that tripped over a stone. She dropped on the icy wet ground, crumbling with pain. A woman behind her stumbled over the fallen body and fell on top of her.

There was no time to check to verify who that miserable woman was or to help her recover and to stand up and continue to walk again. We tripped over the body as if we were blind, and we were. We became blind to another human fellow and continued to walk as if nothing happened.

The SS helped to end the woman's suffering. He hoisted his stick up in the air and landed it on her head. It was an improved leather stick with additional iron ball on its top. The iron ball cut her scalp, and then there was silence, a scary silence. The woman died immediately. We did not stop to see who she was. We just continued to walk, fearful for our own lives.

I still remember the sound of the hitting, the sound of the iron ball cracking the head, *Mom moaned.* it still churns my stomach, the sound of it.

We continued to walk, a group of desperate and exhausted skins and bones following the right German order. And then another woman collapsed, slithered into a melted snowy puddle. She did not suffer for long. The SS pulled the trigger and shot her head. It was a direct hit on the target. The SS finished her feeble suffering, killing the frail woman to prevent interruption. They completed their tasks with the least amount of bullets.

We continued to walk thoughtlessly, each woman mindlessly following yet aware of her own tender, fragile existence. All I cared about was to continue to walk and to help my sister carry on. She was worn-out. I needed her alive, and she knew that. I held her arm, assisting her to shuffle her swollen feet. She leaned over my arm, and so we passed step after step in a horror march, the death march.

We arrived in a small village, heading toward a barn in a farm for the night's rest. An order was given: eat the bread. We ate the bread and licked the melted snowflakes with our palms shaking.

We continued our journey the following morning. Several other groups were ahead of us in the front. We did not look at the other walking skeletons. We just observed the frozen bodies on the roadsides as we passed. The roadsides were covered with the feeble that were not able to continue. Some were still alive, taking their last few breaths.

We were given orders to stop on several occasions. The SS needed time to get reorganized, to exchange people, to replace the tired SS. New officers arrived, riding motorcycles. And we loved those breaks. We were left alone for a few minutes. We sat on the freezing ground, eating and licking the melted snow.

We walked day after day, surviving, thriving, and hoping for news, for good news. At night, we slept in farmers' barns. We were surprised at night when local villagers, endangering their own life, would sneak to the barn, leaving food—buckets of soup, cabbage, potatoes, bread. The precious food was quickly consumed.

We did not know where we were heading.

A new group of women merged with our convoy, spreading rumors about the German evacuation and abandonment of the concentration camps. They saw with their own eyes the Germans' destruction of evidence, the burning of camps while evacuating the skeletons. They witnessed the Germans killing political prisoners and the feeblest that could not walk anymore.

German vehicles passed us. Three-wheel motorcycles and armored trucks loaded with soldiers. They were all storming forward and leaving only mud lines behind.

We soon learned that we were moving toward the German border but were not sure whether it was a good sign or the end of our existence.

We stopped at the train station only a few kilometers from the border and prepared for sleeping. We stretched out on the ground and covered ourselves with cots that were thrown to us from an army supply truck that had passed by.

At dusk, we prepared to continue the march toward the train station. There was an old locomotive attached to several cattle wagons waiting, ready for the human convoy. The SS officers were pushing us with rifle butts, hurrying to walk faster. They were very careful not to touch prisoners with their hands, always afraid of Jewish germs and spreading typhus that killed so many.

We did not know to where we were heading. Our last voyage in the same cattle wagons was our initial transport to Auschwitz. There was no clue, nor that it mattered. We turned into apathetic human beings.

Fifty women fit in a small wagon, fifty skeletons sitting and standing in a small wagon that fits five cows at the most. My sister was at my side, and that was all that mattered. I held her hand, and we felt inseparable.

We exchanged standing spots, reaching out for more air to breathe. The wagon that was built for delivering cattle had only few small air openings. Only the tallest woman in the cattle wagon could get fresh air. The tallest reported the locations that we passed by, giving details about the changing landscapes outside and reading the road signs.

Woman after woman collapsed on the wagon floor, and there was no space on the wagon floor to lie straight. Bodies were pushed aside, pushed with feet and folded into the corners. At the end of the day, the pile of bodies grew higher, one body on top of the other. At some train stops, we are watered with hoses. The German officers spread water on the outside walls of the wagon, and a few water drops entered in, into the open mouths.

At other train stops, the wagon doors were opened with the strong SS hands. The SS commanded us to remove the fallen bodies and throw them out. It was our duty to lift each body and dump it in on the roadside. We picked up the lifeless bodies and hoisted them to the field.

A sudden sharp whistle cut the air. We were pushed back to the wagon. It was less crowded. The locomotive started its engine, and the train continued.

Soon we arrived at the German border. We entered the German ground, passing through army camps, through destroyed villages, and air-raided towns.

We started to believe the rumors.

Heavy snow was covering the deserted houses and the empty villages. Inside the wagon, we stood frozen and exhausted. We already finished the few old breadcrumbs, the provision that we kept from the beginning of the voyage a long time ago. The woman that stood near the small windows extended her arms through the metal bars and collected snowflakes and passed it to another woman who stood at her side. It was passed from woman to woman, from hand to hand. We licked the drops, the melted snowflakes.

The train stopped in a small village. The locomotive engine went silent and died completely. Within a minute, the SS opened the iron doors, cursing the whole world, yelling, ordering to clear the wagon, shnell and quickly.

We crawled down and moved out of the wagon. It was hard to stretch our stiff bones. We marched along the metal rails. My sister's foot was swollen, damaged from walking and from standing. She leaned on my arm, hardly able to bear a few more steps.

The SS was yelling, raging with frustration, hurling the convoy toward the nearest house. We entered into a barn. A smell of fresh straws that was just cut mellowed the pain as if promising possible rest and comfort. Chickens were walking freely in the barn, searching for seeds, and we envied them. They were free in life and had free food.

Behind the barn, there was a partly frozen pond, and it was promising. *Mom's voice faded away as if she was suspended in the experience, feeling again those moments.*

The SS, busying with their own matters, left us for a while to settle, allowing a little time for organizing, resting in the barn. My sister stretched her body, lying on straw, unable to move even one step further. I headed straight to the pond, imagining the water flushing my body. Within a few seconds, I stripped my clothes. My body was craving for water to flush the dirt and the aches. We had not bathed since we left the camp. I jumped into the freezing pond, not thinking, not caring, just feeling the freezing water purifying my heart and feeling alive again.

I was the only woman in the water.

An old German man walked silently toward the barn. He was leaning on a walking wood cane and sneaked a small bag full of dry pieces of bread.

It was heavenly bread, *shavertzbroiten,* dark brown homemade bread. I can still remember its taste, *Mom sighed. She loved dark German bread. "They knew how to bake a good dark bread," she used to say years later when she taught me how to search for a good dark bread from the bakery shelf. It was my duty every Friday morning before school started to buy dark bread "well baked," along with two challah breads for Shabbat, at the bakery in the main street of Bennie Barak.*

It was a real fresh German dark bread, *Mom continued, and it amazed me how a person can have good memories from such a dark time in life.*

We continued the march on the following morning. The SS hurried the convoy toward the train station. My sister was sick and weak. Her foot was swollen and covered with frostbite. I supported her back, and with the help of another woman, she continued forward.

We arrived at the station and saw other groups of skeletons, emaciated women, standing and waiting for the unknown. It was as if we were seeing ourselves in a mirror, seeing desperation and wasted bodies watching us.

A sudden, sharp whistle cut the air. A locomotive carrying a line of wagons arrived at the station. The SS came with a new order: "Selection," ordering the group into a long line for another selection.

"Am I going to lose my sister now?" I asked myself, *Mom remembered.* I did not want to lose her after all that we had been through.

Rumors circulated that we were toward the northwestern station of Germany and that the Germans were losing the war with the Russians.

15

Final Destination
Bergen-Belsen

The train passed through German villages and stopped for fueling and for removing dead bodies. We turned into experts in removing bodies, holding hands and legs, lifting up the body, and throwing it gently on the ground, but not before stripping the bodies of valuable clothing. At each stop, the space in the wagon got bigger. The selection in each stop continued also. We stood in rows of five, facing the wagon, and the SS, thrilled to finish with the half-dead prisoners, passed between the rows, checking the skeletons, the worn—out women. Those that only few months ago were healthy and normal had now turned into shadows of themselves.

The SS investigated the skeletons. They pushed and poked the bodies with rifle butts, checking for any residual of strength. They pressed backs, shoulders, and spread apart legs.

A fall to the ground was an ultimate death sentence. Women that fell to the ground were pushed aside and were shot to death. The SS did not hesitate to pull the trigger. They did it eagerly. The German order was to get rid of any possible distraction.

My sister's condition continued to deteriorate. She was ready to give up but desperately feared every selection. I continued to live for her and needed her to continue, to survive for me. *Mom's voice faded. I know what will come next, and I pulled out the old saying "you did your best. You fought to preserve her life. You were a brave sister," and Mom continued.*

"Ken," *she always said in Hebrew*, "Yes, and it is still painful, it will always be. To lose my sister. I was not able to save her. The horror, the fear, and the pain, all these suffering. And I did not care. I just wanted to keep her alive. The only thing that mattered was my sister Yocheved."

The heavy snow continued to fall day and night. It froze us inside the wagon. Every night, the train stopped for refueling and selection. The SS were thrilled to rid of the finished and even more excited to reduce the number of the unproductive ones.

Food was even more scarce than before. At some stops, we received a few pieces of bread from local villagers, from those that felt pity and wanted to help. And for every piece of bread, there was a struggle. The women, like starving animals, fought over every discarded piece of food. Every breadcrumb was crucial. It was a real life savior. We dipped the pieces of bread in snowflakes. In other stops, we received only yelling and scolding, and we stayed hungry.

The train passed through German villages, and at each stop, we gained new knowledge about the situation at the front lines. Rumors abounded about the Germans' defeat and the Russians moving forward the German borders. The hope of escape was interweaving with the hunger and the death.

We arrived in Belsen.

The train stopped for several hours at the Belsen train station. Dead bodies were shoveled out along with a roll call to verify the number of women that were left in the group. The train continued for several more kilometers, and a big sign covered with snow declared "Bergen-Belsen Ehrholungslager" (Recovery Camp).

We were ordered to clear the wagon to get into rows of fives. Orders were thrown in the air. New SS commanders were exchanged for the old. The new guards were waiting in the station for the new arrivals. The station was rapidly filled with lines of skeletons, men and women. The men marched on the right, and the women marched on the left.

We moved forward, convoys of skeletons with curved backs and hanging gowns, completely dead tired, walking and supporting one another. I held my sister's arm and pushed us forward. We did not talk. There was no energy to speak, only the bodily understanding of the situation. I touched my sister, knowing that she was still alive.

We craved food, dreamed of bread, imagined soup and potatoes, and hoped to get food in the new camp.

We entered the camp. There were lines of gray barracks, well-familiar scenery of another German camp. We imagined the upcoming comfort inside the barracks. We yearned for the crowded bunks that were stretched from wall to wall, the rough wood that was a real place to lie on, to rest.

We arrived at the camp center and joined the human assembly line that was waiting for selection to "recovery units." The sick and the feeble went to the medical block. The selection went fast. We did not have to strip our clothes. We just walked slowly in front of the "medical" inspectors. Some women were ordered to stand aside, but most of us continued on. My sister followed my steps. We passed again together. We stayed tight and moved fast to the next station. It was the feeding line. And again, we received a small chunk of bread with a warm watery potato soup. Shaking with hunger, we swallowed it immediately.

The line moved forward straight to the showers. There were women standing with ragged clothes in their hands. This was a real shower, and real water streamed out from the iron tubes. The next station was clothing. New gowns and new shoes were distributed. We started to feel human.

We finally marched to the barrack. It was a long one flat building filled with hundreds of bunks, three levels. Women inside were heading for their night's sleep. We walked along a line of beds, desperate to find a spot. The capos shouted out their orders in German, "Seven women at each bunk." We found a vacant spot. My sister crawled first, and I followed her. Believing and not believing our fortune, we curved into each other's body and drifted into a deep sleep.

The first morning at Bergen-Belsen, the "recovery camp," started quiet, with no yelling or shouting. We were left alone and were free to walk, to talk, free to search for familiar faces to learn what happened to relatives.

A voice from the past interrupted my thoughts. It was a familiar voice. I turned around to see who it was, looked at the woman at her face, and did not recognize her.

She said my name, "Rachel, Rachel." It was hard to recognize her, my childhood friend and neighbor from Sighet, Rebecca. She got married to a young rabbi from Budapest a few years before it all started. The chubby little woman, my friend that I knew for years, turned into a small, tiny walking skeleton. Her facial skin was hanging over her cheekbones without flush underneath. Rebecca, the sweetest girl that everybody likes, looked as a half-dead woman.

She called my nickname, "Rushi, Rushi, don't you remember me? I am Rebecca, your friend." She came closer. I saw the sparkle of life in her eyes. I recognized her voice, but her face, her body, changed so much. She was transferred from Sighet to Auschwitz and then to Gross-Rosen. She arrived to Bergen-Belsen only few days prior to us.

Her large family was killed in the crematorium of Auschwitz. She did not know what happened to her husband. He was taken to Auschwitz as all of us and disappeared after the first selection in Birkenau. Rebecca's six-month-old baby boy, Michael, was snatched from her arm and was thrown to a long cart at the first selection in Birkenau. The cart was carried directly to the gas chambers.

Rebecca revealed the horror, the suffering, the body's humiliation. She was held, along with other women, in a separate barrack where the German officers had an easy access to female prisoners' bodies. *Mom gets quiet. She did not want to continue with this story, the story of the Jewish women that were forced to satisfy the desires of the SS. Mom did not want to expound. She tells Rebecca's story in general description as if trying to protect me. Or protecting Rebecca's dignity?*

Rebecca was freed from this horror when she was transferred to Gross-Rosen and then to Bergen-Belsen. Her health was deteriorating. She had a high fever like many other women in the block, and later on, she was sent to the medical block.

Bergen-Belsen was different. Most women in the block were too sick, too weak to move, just surviving day to day. We were allowed to rest the first few days to recover. There were no special plans. We just stretched out on the bunks and talked. We walked in the front yard of the block. News about the German defeat in the fronts was the main issue. We saw signs of the coming end. Some guards were more human, less vicious. There were less rules and orders, less food, less water.

Women died form typhus, dysentery, and starvation. They were too exhausted to withstand the outbreak of epidemic diseases. My sister had a high fever also. She slept on her bunk most of the days. I fed her with small pieces of bread dipped in a watery soup of cabbage or potatoes. She was too sick to swallow. I chewed the bread slowly and cut into smaller pieces and pushed my fingers in between her lips as if feeding a small bird. She could hardly swallow.

My sister was transferred to the medical block. She was unable to walk, and I carried her on my arms. The medical block was filled with dying sick women lying on bunks along with other crowded bodies. There was no doctor, no medication, only nurses carrying dead bodies. It looked like the last station of torture.

I left my sister in the nurse's hands and went back to the barrack. An abrupt and unusual amount of traffic interrupted the slow paces of the camp. SS officers riding on motorcycles and on small cars crossed the main camp. They were packed with army tools and headed toward the main gate.

16

Liberation and Death

The Sixty-Third Anti-Tank Regiment of the British Royal Artillery librated Bergen-Belsen. The date was April 15, 1945, a year after we were deported from our homes in Sighet.

The British soldiers, the Tommy Boys—*Mom remembered their nickname*—were friendly. They looked healthy and normal. It was pleasant to hear their English language, soothing soft words without commands and yelling. They distributed bread and dried crackers. They provided clothing, underwear, pants, shirts, and shoes. We ate and ate, and there was no time to think or to be sad. The only thing that mattered was to fill up the emptied stomachs.

The underwear given by the British army was hidden deep in your underwear drawer for many years after the war. You kept it in the back drawer. You never touched it or talked about it. You did not allow me to see it or touch it. It was as if a big secret lying in the closet, and I was fascinated with "the secret." When you left the house to work, I pulled out the faded pink top undershirt and the silky underwear, the "liberation garments." Captivated with its story, with its smell, and the texture, I patted it carefully and measured it on my body. You never knew about my secret, and you still do not know. These garments were given recently to Yad Vashem, the Holocaust museum in Jerusalem.

The Germans, the SS, the officers, the soldiers, and those who were not successful in leaving before the British arrived were captured and imprisoned by the British. The Germans were forced to manage the dead bodies, to burry the Jews that did not survive, the tortured, the sick that died with typhus.

A few days after the liberation, I got sick with typhus along with many other women in the barrack. It started with a high fever and delirium. I would often drift into and out of consciousness, not knowing where I was. I forgot about my sister and slept days and nights for two weeks.

We were carried out to the hospital, and as I learned later, the Red Cross nurses and doctors took care of us.

After two weeks, I came back to life. When I opened my eyes, I learned what had happened. I was very weak and could hardly walk. I ate very little portions of food.

My sister was not there. She disappeared. I searched for her and asked for help. I begged two volunteers, male nurses, to help in finding my sister. Leaning over the volunteers' arms, we went from one barrack to another. Most barracks were turned into medical units, hospitals.

I found my sister after several days of desperation. It was the last barrack, the medical unit, where she spent her last days. When I asked the nurses whether they had a woman named Yocheved, they looked at one another's faces, hesitating to reveal the truth, but I knew the answer. She died few days earlier while I was drifting in and out of life, fighting for my own survival.

I lost my beloved sister Yocheved.

I could not see Mom's face, but I just imagined her sitting on her simple bed holding the phone silently. I could not touch or hug her. She was too far away, and I did not know what to say. I felt her pain and was sad for myself.

There was nothing to live for anymore, *Mom continued.* I wanted to die too. Life was painful, agonizing, with no family and no brothers, no sisters, all alone in a crazy world, a world of sickness, displacement, orphanhood.

Surviving the horror all by myself was unbearable. It was unclear to me how and why I survived the terror and why my sister did not survived and died a few days after the liberation. I usually wondered what I should have done to keep her alive. What was that I did not do to make sure that she survived with me?

I was taken back to the hospital. My heart was empty with no energy left in it. The Irish volunteer nurses assisted me into the bed. They put me gently on the white bed without leaving my side even for a moment, pouring sips of tea into my mouth and reviving my body.

I returned to life gradually. The British army and the Red Cross provided our necessities. We were not hungry anymore and began to look more human. We gained weight. A strong appetite for life awakened the body. A strong urge for life, to live, carried me forward.

I joined an agency in the camp that helped displaced individuals find family members and survivors. The agency was set up in an empty barrack. It consisted of several chairs and tables that were turned into a center of registration. A matching list of names and addresses was organized in few days. Desperate individuals searching for loved ones were standing in line giving names of relatives, refusing to believe bad news.

It was a recovering task and healing for me. Sisters and brothers in the tragedy surrounded me. I did not feel alone. I was surrounded by people like me, and I immersed my being into doing and making, helping others to regain life.

The Hmador Llchepos Krovim, the "Search for Relatives and Survivors," had become a major part of the family life in Israel. Every evening the house turned silent. There was no talking and no breathing loud. Mother turned the radio on loud, and name after name flowed into the room.

"Maybe tonight we will find a relative or somebody that we knew," you always said. The "Search for Relatives and Survivors" radio program lasted for ten years (1950-1960), but Mom did not find relatives or survivors through the radio.

A list of "Searching for Relatives" was published at the *Unzer Shtimme* (our Voice), the local Jewish paper in Bergen-Belsen. It helped many survivors to find relatives and reunite.

We were transferred to Camp 2 of Bergen Belsen. It was under the authority of the British army. The barracks in the old site of Bergen-Belsen were burned down to combat the typhus epidemic. Several hundreds of people died every day and were buried in a mass grave outside the camp.

My sister Yocheved is buried there. And a big piece of my heart is still there with her.

The Ending Story

After the liberation from evilness, Mom discovered that her brother Jonathan survived the war too. He served in the Hungarian army just as other Jewish young men who were forced to serve did. She found out that he was alive through common friends that came to search for their own relatives in the agency of Bergen-Belsen. Jonathan was thin and exhausted but recovered fast and even got married soon after the liberation as many other single men and women who desired to rejuvenate their life did.

Mom traveled back home to see what was left from her life. She traveled on a train that was loaded with Polish and Hungarian villagers. One of the villagers who did not like to see a Jewish woman sitting next to them made a remark, "I thought that they were all killed." Mom did not hesitate and responded, "There are many other survivors like me, and you will have to put up with it, and now is your turn to suffer." The woman that made the remark moved from sitting next to Mom to another place, far away.

It was sad to see the destruction of Sighet. She found the house populated by a Hungarian family. They did not allow Mom to enter the house. Mom recognized the changes through the entrance door. The family that occupied the house removed the family pictures from the wall, snatched the mezuzah from the door lintel, and destroyed every sign of Jewish existence from the house. It was not home anymore.

Mom returned to Bergen-Belsen and reunited with Shemual, an old friend from Budapest. They got married, and a beautiful healthy baby girl was born.

The small family moved to Israel in 1948, and I was born a few years later.

Rachel, my mom, is eighty-eight years old now and lives in a nursing home in Israel. Mom is healthy and content with life. She has two daughters, grandchildren, and great-grandchildren.

I was asked to write Mom's story. It was her dream to tell the story, to reveal the love, the longing for her sister Yocheved.

I was named after Yocheved, Mom's sister who died few days after liberation.

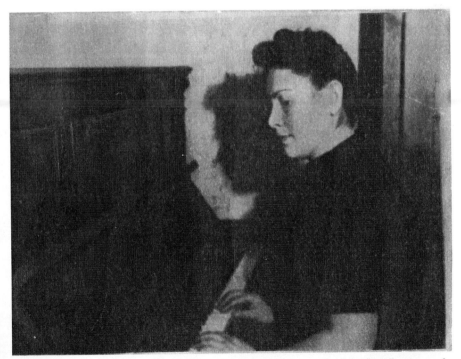

Rachel, my mother, six years after the war ended in Haifa, Israel.
April, 1951